Sarah Hudelson

Write On

Language in Education
Theory and Practice

Write On
Children Writing in ESL

Sarah Hudelson

A publication of ![CAL] Center for Applied Linguistics

Prepared by the ERIC Clearinghouse on Languages and Linguistics

Prentice Hall Regents Englewood Cliffs, New Jersey 07632

Library of Congress Cataloging-in-Publication Data

Hudelson, Sarah.
    Write on : children writing in ESL / Sarah Hudelson.
    128 pp. — (Language in education ; 72)
    "A publication of Center for Applied Linguistics prepared by the
  Clearinghouse on Languages and Linguistics."
    Bibliography: p. 99
    ISBN 0-13-891961-5
    1. English language—Study and teaching—Foreign speakers.
  2. English language—Composition and exercises—Study and teaching.
  3. Language arts. I. Center for Applied Linguistics. II. ERIC
  Clearinghouse on Languages and Linguistics. III. Title.
  IV. Series.
  PE1128.A2H83   1989
  372.65'21044—dc20   89-8662
                                                                                                            CIP

Language in Education: Theory and Practice 72

This publication was prepared with funding from the Office of Educational Research and Improvement, U.S. Department of Education, under contract No. RI 88062010. The opinions expressed in this report do not necessarily reflect the positions or policies of OERI or ED.

Production and editorial supervision: Janet S. Johnston
Manufacturing buyer: Mike Woerner
Cover design: Celine A. Grandes of Photo Plus Art

© 1989 by the Center for Applied Linguistics
and by Prentice Hall Regents,
a Division of Simon & Schuster
Englewood Cliffs, New Jersey 07632

All rights reserved. No part of this book may be reproduced, in any form or by any means, without permission in writing from the publisher.

Printed in the United States of America

10 9 8 7 6 5 4 3 2

ISBN 0-13-891961-5

Prentice-Hall International (UK) Limited, *London*
Prentice-Hall of Australia Pty. Limited, *Sydney*
Prentice-Hall Canada Inc., *Toronto*
Prentice-Hall Hispanoamericana, S.A., *Mexico*
Prentice-Hall of India Private Limited, *New Delhi*
Prentice-Hall of Japan, Inc., *Tokyo*
Simon & Schuster Asia Pte. Ltd., *Singapore*
Editora Prentice-Hall do Brasil, Ltda., *Rio de Janeiro*

Contents

Introduction	1
CHAPTER 1: Children's Writing: Native Language and ESL Perspectives	5
The Cognitive Perspective on Native Language Writing	6
The Social Perspective on Native Language Writing	13
The Cultural Perspective on Native Language Writing	16
The Cognitive Perspective on ESL Writing	20
The Social Perspective on ESL Writing	23
The Cultural Perspective on ESL Writing	33
CHAPTER 2: The Place of Native Language Writing in ESL Writing Development	37
CHAPTER 3: Writing Instruction for the Elementary ESL Student: Applications from Research	47
Expressive Writing	51
Poetic Writing and the Reading/Writing Connection	59
Transactional Writing	67
CHAPTER 4: Assessing Children's Writing	79
Writing Assessment and the Classroom Teacher	80
Writing Assessment and the Child	90
Conclusion	98
References	99

Language in Education
Theory and Practice

ERIC (Educational Resources Information Center) is a nationwide network of information centers, each resposible for a given educational level or field of study. ERIC is supported by the Office of Educational Research and Improvement of the U.S. Department of Education. The basic objective of ERIC is to make current developments in educational research, instruction, and personnel preparation readily accessible to educators and members of related professions.

ERIC/CLL is the ERIC Clearinghouse of Languages and Linguistics, one of the specialized clearinghouses in the ERIC system, and is operated by the Center for Applied Linguistics (CAL). ERIC/CLL is specifically responsible for the collection and dissemination of information on research in languages and linguistics and its application to language teaching and learning.

The ERIC Clearinghouse on Languages and Linguistics (ERIC/CLL) publishes two monographs each year under the series title, *Language in Education: Theory and Practice*. ERIC/CLL commissions specialists to write about current issues in the fields of languages and linguistics. The series includes practical guides, state-of-the-art papers, theoretical reviews, and collected reports. The publications are intended for use by educators, researchers, and others interested in language education.

This publication can be purchased directly from Prentice Hall Regents and will be available from the ERIC Document Reproduction Service, Alexandria, Virginia.

For further information on the ERIC system, ERIC/CLL, and CAL/ Clearinghouse publications, write to ERIC Clearinghouse on Languages and Linguistics, Center for Applied Linguistics, 1118 22nd Street, NW, Washington, DC 20037.

Whitney Stewart, Editor, Language in Education

About the Author

Sarah Hudelson is Associate Professor in the Division of Curriculum and Instruction at Arizona State University. She is a former Associate Professor in the Department of Teaching and Learning at the University of Miami, and a former elementary school teacher, having worked in migrant and bilingual classrooms in Texas and Michigan. Dr. Hudelson received her PhD from the University of Texas at Austin and has worked in bilingual/second language teacher education in Texas, Arizona, and Florida. Dr. Hudelson's research interests are in the area of bilingual children's first and second language literacy development, and she has published in journals such as *TESOL Quarterly*, *NABE Journal*, *Language Arts*, and *The Reading Teacher*. Dr. Hudelson is particularly concerned that professionals in language education, whether they work in native language settings or in bilingual or second language programs, work together to facilitate learners' linguistic and intellectual growth.

Acknowledgments

I am grateful to several people who have contributed, directly or indirectly, to this effort. I offer my thanks to the following people: to the anonymous reviewers who provided helpful comments and suggestions on an earlier draft of the manuscript; to Whitney Stewart, editor at the ERIC Clearinghouse on Languages and Linguistics, who both encouraged me and kept me on task; and to special colleagues who, over the years, have nourished, supported, and taught me about learning and language learning. I thank particularly: Carole Edelsky, D. Scott Enright, Judith Lindfors, Mary Lou McCloskey, Mary Jane Nations, Pat Rigg, Katharine Samway and Carole Urzua.

I also thank my husband, Donald Vance, who sustains me professionally with his unwavering confidence in my abilities, and personally through his unconditional love and acceptance.

Write On

Introduction

Twenty-five years ago elementary school teachers working in English as a second language (ESL) settings probably would have received the following advice with regard to the teaching of writing:

> Don't worry about teaching writing until the children have mastered the oral language. Teach children to understand and to speak English first. Language develops sequentially from listening to speaking to reading, and finally to writing. Writing is the last of the language processes to develop, and it is the hardest for children to master. Therefore, writing is the last of the language processes to be taught. Elementary ESL educators should focus on developing children's speaking vocabularies and not concentrate on literacy.

Today, as will become obvious in this volume, the advice given to teachers is quite different. Instead of advocating an almost exclusive focus on oral language, teachers are urged to provide young second language learners with early and continued reading and writing experiences. Practices similar to those suggested for native speakers of English are recommended, and the perspective taken is that all of the language processes develop simultaneously and interdependently. How did this change in viewpoint come about? What has occurred to bring about such a change in approach?

In the last quarter of a century, a significant amount of child language research has been carried out. The findings of many of these studies have influenced educators' views of children's developing language abilities. The earliest pioneering work examined children's oral language acquisition and altered the commonly held view that children learned through imitation of adult models and through mimicry. Instead, language development researchers have concluded that children are active participants in an ongoing process of figuring out how language works, that children are in control of the process of language acquisition. There is presently evidence for language educators to make several assertions about children's language acquisition:

1) As humans, children seem predisposed to acquire language.

2) Children's intellectual tasks in language learning involve figuring out how the language works, that is, structuring the language for themselves, which they do by making and testing hypotheses about the language and gradually refining these hypotheses over time. Children are also involved in learning how to use language to fulfill their own intentions and in learning how to use language appropriately in the varied social settings in which they find themselves. Children focus jointly on linguistic and communicative aims (Lindfors, 1987).

3) Language acquisition is a social as well as a cognitive enterprise. Language development does not occur in a vacuum; other people play an important role. Children develop as language users through interacting with others who respond to their efforts to use language and who "teach" them language within the context of daily activities. Language acquisition must be seen from the perspective of social interaction (Bruner, 1981; Lindfors, 1987; Wells, 1986).

4) Within different cultural groups, there are different ways of interacting with infants and young children, so that there is no one "best" way that adults and peers serve as language teachers. Also, as children grow within their own communities, they become competent communicators within a particular setting, and communities differ in their definitions of what makes a successful or competent communicator. Cultural variation must always be considered when talking about language acquisition and possible language acquisition universals (Heath, 1983; Ochs & Schieffelen, 1983).

Influenced at least in part by studies in first language acquisition, researchers began to investigate the processes by which children learned their second language. Researchers have discovered that the processes of first and second language acquisition in children are more alike than different. Giving particular emphasis to the setting of the school, researchers have made the following conclusions about children's second language development:

1) Second language learners are actively engaged in figuring out the rules for the language they are learning. The process of second language acquisition is essentially a process of creative construction of the new language. Through ongoing experimentation, second language learners generate the rules of the new language (Dulay & Burt, 1974; Ellis, 1985; Lindfors, 1987).

2) Errors are a natural and essential part of second language acquisition (Ellis, 1985).

3) There are significant individual differences in rates of acquisition of English as a second language, as well as in attitudes toward the new language and its speakers (Fillmore, 1976, 1983).

4) Second language learners want and need to use the new language (as they have already learned to use their native language) to accomplish their purposes and to express their intentions. Within the framework of individual differences, they work hard, employing various strategies, in order to be included in ongoing activities (Cathcart-Strong, 1986; Fillmore, 1976; Ventriglia, 1982).

5) Both adults and peers offer important "teacher" functions that provide both comprehensible input and motivation to continue developing English (Ellis, 1985; Enright, 1986; Fillmore, 1976).

6) Children's cultural backgrounds may have an effect on their second language learning, in terms of such diverse factors as participant structures and rules for talking and understanding how school is conducted (Au, 1980; Fillmore, 1986; Philips, 1983).

In both first and second language settings, research on oral language acquisition has led naturally to investigations of children's literacy development. Research on children's writing thus takes place within the larger framework of, and is also an integral part of, the broad field of language acquisition and development. As will become evident, research on the acquisition of writing by children reaches conclusions that are quite similar to the findings of studies on the acquisition of spoken language. Young writers, whether in their native language or in a second language, creatively construct written language and develop their understanding of writing within their homes, communities, and schools.

An understanding of the creative, problem-solving nature of the writing process, and of the social and cultural contexts in which writing ability develops, helps teachers to see the implications for and applications to classroom practice. The first two chapters of this monograph review some of the recent research on children's first and second language writing, including the influence of native language reading and writing ability on ESL writing development. Chapters three and four consider the application of research to instructional strategies and the need for classroom assessment and documentation of children's progress as writers. The aim of the volume is to provide teachers with an overview of research and theory about ESL children's writing, from the perspective that research and theory may and should inform practice.

1

Children's Writing: Native Language and ESL Perspectives

The topic of this volume is writing, specifically the writing development of young English as a second language (ESL) learners. Elementary schools view writing as one of the language arts, and in the last fifteen to twenty years, elementary education researchers and educators have given considerable attention both to understanding how children develop as writers and to facilitating children becoming proficient at the writer's craft. Information is available not only from native English-speaking children (see Bissex, 1980; Calkins, 1983, 1986; Dyson, 1984; Graves, 1983; Harste, Woodward & Burke, 1984), but also from native speakers of other languages, such as Spanish (Edelsky, 1986; Edelsky & Jilbert, 1986; Ferreiro & Teberosky, 1982; Hudelson, 1981-1982) and Japanese (Kitagawa & Kitagawa, 1987). In recent years, ESL educators have given more attention to literacy development, recognizing that students need to be able to read and write effectively if they are going to be successful in English language classrooms (Allen, 1986; Hudelson, 1984; Urzua, 1987b).

Berthoff (1981) has defined writing as an act of the mind by which writers create meaning. This monograph will use Berthoff's definition, that writing is the creating of meaning from one's own intellectual and linguistic resources and activity, rather than the copying of someone else's text, or the use of prepared lists of words to create sentences or stories. Using this definition as a base, the first part of this chapter will examine current information on the writing development of native English-speaking children. The second part of the chapter will do the same for the writing development of ESL children.

In a 1987 paper published in *Written Communication,* Carolyn Piazza identifies and categorizes what she calls context variables in writing research. Piazza demonstrates that writing has been and is currently being examined from various perspectives or contexts. She outlines three major contexts: the cognitive, the social, and the cultural. The cognitive perspective focuses on what the individual writer does during writing, on strategies and processes that the individual uses in the production of a text, on what the writer brings to the writing task, and on what some features of the text might be. The social perspective considers the role and influence of others (for example, parents, teacher, and peers) and the influence of the social setting (for example, home and school) on the individual writer and on the text produced. The cultural perspective emphasizes the ways in which the writer's membership in a particular cultural group may affect not only written products but also the writer's ideas about what writing is, what it is for, what should be written, and so on. For both native speakers and second language learners, the research reviewed in this chapter will be considered from these three perspectives.

The Cognitive Perspective on Native Language Writing

Beginning Writing

It is becoming increasingly evident that young children in print-oriented or print-saturated societies, long before they enter school or receive formal literacy instruction, interact with print, make hypotheses about how the written language works, and engage in reading and writing behaviors (Ferreiro & Teberosky, 1982; Harste, Woodward & Burke, 1984). Children come to school having experimented with writing, having created texts, and able to read those texts to themselves and to someone else (Goodman & Goodman, 1979). As they do with oral language, children change their hypotheses about written language (and therefore, their writing) to reflect their changing interpretations. Even their unconventional efforts make clear that children are writers who have specific intentions to create meaning through written texts (Harste, Woodward & Burke, 1984).

In a detailed case study, Baghban (1984) traced the writing and reading development of her daughter, Giti. Baghban discovered that by about 18 months her daughter was creating written products that to an adult eye looked like scribbles. Yet, Giti labeled these writings, informing her mother that she was writing names of familiar people and objects. Giti continued to write, and before age three she was creating such diverse texts as grocery lists and thank you letters to her grandmother. She could and did read these texts to interested adults. While an adult would not recognize letters or even letter-like forms in these texts, it was easy to see that the grocery list resembled an adult's cursive writing or jotting down of a list in a vertical column, while the letter resembled a text made up of sentences written horizontally across the page, also done in cursive. Giti demonstrated that even though she was not using English letters to construct her texts, she was aware of at least two different purposes or functions of writing (to retain something in memory and to fulfill a social obligation); she was aware that different kinds of writing were used to carry out the functions; she knew that she needed to use graphic forms to represent words; and she was willing to generate and test her hypotheses about text and, thus, take the risk to create these texts.

Bissex (1980) also conducted a case study, following her son, Paul's, writing and reading development through the age of five. Bissex discovered that, as did Giti, Paul used writing for a variety of different purposes of personal importance to him, including attempting to regulate the behavior of others with a sign over his workbench that read DO NAT DSTRB GNYS AT WRK (Do not disturb Genius at work).

While Baghban and Bissex looked closely at one English-speaking child, Clay (1975) looked at the early writing of many New Zealand preschoolers, discovering patterns across children. Clay documented young children's early and continued experimentation with writing, noting that young writers attached meaning to what adults thought of as sticks and circles or scribble writing. Clay found that the texts produced by many children took similar forms as their understandings about written text changed over time.

Harste, Woodward, and Burke (1984) studied a group of three- to six-year-old children in an effort to learn about the children's concepts of writing (and reading) over time. They found that by age three many of the children already distinguished writing from drawing, using different kinds of strokes for one as contrasted to the other. They documented that between the ages of three to six, children's concepts of writing changed. Their writing became ever more adult-like and conventional looking, according to adult standards. They also found that even at age three children had intentions when they wrote; they could and would interpret what they were doing. As children became older, their writing displayed more and more knowledge of the structures of different genres of writing, so that the lists, maps, notes, letters, and stories that they wrote looked different from one another. The researchers noted that the children, as members of families and communities, had available to them social ways of organizing print. The children learned these ways and then used them in their writing. Finally, Harste, Woodward, and Burke characterized the children as risk-takers, noting that they were willing to construct sentences on the basis of their current operating hypotheses about the nature of written language. The younger children were more willing risk takers than the older informants.

Sulzby (1986) studied writing samples from twenty-four kindergarten children. In a one-to-one setting, she asked children to write her a story and then to read and discuss the story. Analyzing the writing, she found that children created text using six major strategies: writing through drawing; writing through scribbling; writing using letter-like forms (that is, using forms that looked somewhat like conventional letters); writing using well-learned units (for example, using the letters in the child's name and reordering them to spell different words); writing using invented spelling (unconventional spelling based on the child's predictions of spelling); and writing using conventional English spelling.

Investigations also have been carried out with native speakers of languages other than English. Ferreiro and Teberosky (1982) worked with a group of native Spanish speakers from a variety of socioeconomic classes in Mexico City. By giving the children a series of tasks, the researchers discovered that the children made hypotheses about how written language worked and looked, and that these hypotheses changed over time. What children believed about written language at a particular point in time was reflected in the writing they produced. Ferreiro and Teberosky classified the children as falling into one of five stages of writing development.

The writers labeled as being at *Level 1* wrote by making wavy lines or combinations of lines and circles, and by writing larger if they were representing a large person or object in contrast to something smaller. At *Level 2*, children wrote with letter-like forms. In contrast to *Level 1*, children demonstrated that they understood that different meanings must be written differently by using the same set of forms in different arrangements. At *Level 3*, the children hypothesized that each spoken syllable of a word was represented by a letter or letter form. Therefore, they would write the word *gato* (a two-syllable word meaning *cat*) using two-letter forms, and the word *gatito* (the diminutive form of *gato* meaning *little cat*) with three-letter forms. At *Level 4*, children began to use letters of the alphabet, but each letter represented a syllable rather than a sound. At *Level 5*, children employed alphabetic writing, using written characters to represent sounds rather than syllables. Children made use of the alphabetic principle, creating text based on the hypothesis that letters represent speech sounds and that writers create text by relating a stream of speech sounds to particular letters. Flores, Garcia, Gonzalez, Hidalgo, Kaczmarek, and Romero (1985) applied the same scheme to kindergarten Spanish-speaking and English-speaking bilingual children in the United States and discovered that children moved through the same levels.

These changing hypotheses about written language may seem amusing or charming to an adult, but their real significance is that they demonstrate young children's awareness of written language. This awareness includes the concept that talk may be represented in written form. The writing samples also demonstrate that young children are actively engaged in trying to figure out how written language works, and that their hypotheses change as they experience written language. Thus, children learn about written language and how it works through using written language, that is, as they write, as they experiment with written forms, and as they make written language work for them (Harste, Woodward & Burke, 1984).

Invented Spelling

The preceding examples have illustrated that hypothesis-testing and problem-solving begin long before children create text using what Ferreiro and Teberosky call the alphabetic hypothesis or principle. Even as children move into alphabetic writing, they do not automatically write conventionally according to adult standard forms. Rather, they create or invent the spelling of words they do not know how to spell conventionally. In order to invent spellings, children make predictions about how to spell words based on their knowledge of letter names, of letter-sound correspondences, of sounds that are more perceptible in words, of how sounds are pronounced phonetically, and of visual memory word shape. Thus, for example, a child may spell the word *was* as *wuz*, predicting the spelling of the word from prior knowledge of experiences with sound-letter correspondences. That same child may write *thig* for *think*, not producing the *n* because it is less perceptible in the word than the final sound, and substituting a *g* for a *k* because the sounds represented by the two letters are pronounced at the same place in the throat. Children use the alphabetic principle, but they do not limit themselves to conventional sound-letter correspondences (Read, 1971, 1975).

A young child opens his story with: WATSAPATATAYM, and the adult struggles to figure out what the child means. Finally, it becomes clear that the child has written *Once upon a time*. The child has invented spelling, using working hypotheses about letter names, phonetic pronunciations, and salient sounds. The child has even predicted that this conventional opening to a story should be written without any segmentation between words (Harste, Woodward & Burke, 1984). All of this makes clear that the child is actively constructing the written language and then using that construction in the creation of a written message. Even when they use the alphabet, then, children continue to experiment with written language; they continue to hypothesize about the written language; they continue to use what they know at a given point in time to solve their writing problems; they continue to grow in their knowledge of written language by using it to communicate their meanings. This kind of creative construction (Dulay & Burt, 1974) has been documented in native Spanish speakers as well as native speakers of English (Edelsky, 1986; Hudelson, 1981-1982).

Drawing and Writing

Another area of interest for researchers has been the drawing that often accompanies written texts. Investigators have suggested that drawing forms another strategy used by children to discover and create meaning in writing. In his work with first, second, and third graders, Graves (1983, 1984) observed that many children used drawing as an integral part of writing. Some children consistently drew before they wrote, so that drawing became a form of pre-writing or rehearsal for the written text that was to follow. In contrast, some children drew after they wrote, using drawing as illustration; still others moved back and forth between drawing and writing, using both forms of expression, one influencing the other. Calkins (1986) has suggested that, for many writers, drawing as a form of expression may be even more important than writing itself. Dyson (1987) has referred to drawing as the use of another symbolic form, noting that children will use drawing to add on to or clarify written text.

Dyson (1982) has also examined children's talk during composing. She has found, as Smith (1982) maintains, that for many children writing is not a silent activity. Rather, it is accompanied by talk. Children comment on what they are drawing and writing; they ask questions of others; they read or reread during writing; they consider what they will draw and/or write next. Talk may be directed to others or to oneself, in a kind of self-coaching or self-directing activity of figuring out what to create. Thus, a child's talk supports and facilitates a child's writing. Children use talk as a way of working out their text creation (Calkins, 1986; Graves, 1983, 1984).

Narrative Writing

Children's individual struggles to create narratives have also been studied by Calkins (1983, 1986) and Graves (1983, 1984). They have documented some of the ways in which children choose a writing topic, rehearse and draft one version of a piece, reconsider the contents of that piece, and make substantive changes in it before editing the work for form. Calkins and Graves have demonstrated that children can and do reflect on their written products, that children can and do take an audience into account and make substantive changes in pieces based on the comments of others, that children can and do consider and weigh alternative ways of expressing their intentions. Calkins and Grave's research, along with that of many others, has made it clear that child composers share much with older and adult writers who are also working to create texts, or to express or create meaning in written form (Emig, 1971; Flower & Hayes, 1981; Perl, 1979).

Influenced by Reading

This section of chapter one began with the assertion that children in print-oriented societies interact with print and engage in reading as well as writing behaviors before formal schooling begins. Many of children's earliest experiences are with labels on household items, and with familiar print in the environment such as stop signs and McDonald's logos (Goodman & Altwerger, 1981). Children are also involved with connected discourse in written language, written language that includes books, magazines, newspapers, brochures, pamphlets, lists, and letters. Through repeated observations of and personal experiences with different kinds of reading material, children come to understand that people read different kinds of material for different purposes. They also come to understand that print carries meaning and that print makes sense (Goodman, 1986; Teale, 1986). This understanding influences children to write different kinds of texts for different purposes (Baghban, 1984; Harste, Woodward & Burke, 1984).

For many children, but not all, one specific context in which reading behavior emerges (Teale & Sulzby, 1986) is storybook reading. As adults share books with children, children learn both how to handle books and what the elements of story are. Through these experiences children also become aware that the print in books carries the message that the adult is reading (Goodman, 1986). This awareness leads children to attend closely to the written language of stories, to read together with an adult and, eventually, to read without adult assistance. As children's reading comes to approximate closely the language of the story, children become more and more aware of such principles as directionality, and they begin to understand the concepts of word and letter. Through their requests for specific information about words and letters, they receive further information about the written systems of the language, which they then use in their own experiments with reading and writing (Doake, 1985). Children's knowledge of reading, then, provides them with data that they use as they construct meaning in writing.

All the previously discussed aspects of writing affirm that, even for young children, the act of creating text is a cognitive one; children are problem-solving when creating meaning in written form (Teale & Sulzby, 1986). The evidence also suggests that the child actively controls the process, the child figures out what is to be written, the child makes predictions about what form the writing should take, the child takes risks to create the text, and the child uses accumulated prior knowledge about the world of print. The child acts upon the environment. The child is engaged in resolving this problem: how do I create a text that will express what I intend?

The Social Perspective on Native Language Writing

It is very clear, as has already been suggested, that writers, like talkers, do not develop in a vacuum. Writers come to understand writing, and they work at producing texts within a social context. That context may include home and the world at large, as well as the school and classroom.

Returning briefly to the example of Baghban's daughter, Giti, and Bissex's son, Paul, one understands that children's early and continued explorations with writing need to be placed within the context of home environments where adults write and read for many different reasons, where the children see writing and reading take place, and where children are encouraged to write and to read. Giti and Paul used the social context surrounding them both as demonstrations of authentic writing events and as sources of information about the written word (Smith, 1982). The children learned about writing because the demonstrations they witnessed engaged them; they saw how writing was done (Smith, 1982). The children's parents, in turn, responded to their children's explorations with writing. Parents indicated that they recognized, appreciated, and supported their children's intentions as writers. This adult responsiveness is reminiscent of the adult's working to support the child's early efforts to talk. Most probably, this recognition and support had an effect on the children's continued interest in exploring writing and in risking acting on their hypotheses about the written system of English.

The social context for literacy is not necessarily limited to the family. From the perspectives of the wider community, it has become increasingly obvious that children growing up in urban environments around the world are surrounded, from a very early age, by print of various kinds, including print in the environment and on television. Given a human predisposition to make sense of incoming stimuli in their world, children, once they become aware of this print, work to make sense of it. As noted earlier, this sense-making includes using information gleaned from reading the written language in their own writing samples.

The School Setting and Writing

The school is another social context for writing, and one that is critical for children in many ways. Some investigators have examined the school setting as a context for writing, focusing on the kinds of writing students are asked to do, the purposes for which students write, and audiences for the writing. Influential studies of writing in secondary schools have shown that most forms of writing produced at school are done in an expository tone that responds to questions or completes an assignment. Most writing is done to prove to the teacher that an assignment has been completed or that the student has understood certain material. Children learn that the teacher's role is to correct the papers that are turned in (Britton, Burgess, Martin, McLeod, & Rosen, 1975; Applebee, Auten, & Lehr, 1981).

One significant implication of this work is that participating in these kinds of writing assignments gives students certain impressions: that writing is done for someone and not for oneself; that the basic function of writing is to display one's knowledge to someone else; that writing consists of displaying one's knowledge by the use of specific structures and forms; that teachers know what those forms and structures are; and that it is the teacher's job to make sure that student writing conforms to those forms. This is a very different view of the writing process from the one suggested by Berthoff (1981) and many others, where the focus is on writing as a process of discovery, where writing is used as a way of working through what one means, and where the audience for writing (both teachers and peers) responds primarily to the writer's attempts to create meaning rather than to the forms and structures used.

Similarly, studies of writing in elementary schools have shown that, in many school settings, writing is a matter of filling in the blanks, of using someone else's choices to create stories for the teacher, or of proving to the teacher that an assignment was understood and accomplished (Florio & Clark, 1982; Dyson, 1984). Instead of learning to write, children learn how to negotiate school tasks, how to *do* school (Dyson, 1984). As Smith (1982) has noted, the way in which writing is practiced in many classrooms may leave young writers with the impression that writing is essentially getting things down "correctly" in a conventional fashion (what Smith calls transcription), rather than being the act of choosing ideas and creating a text to represent those ideas (what Smith calls composition).

Teachers' assumptions about writing and the teaching of writing have an effect on what is taught, on how it is taught, and on what the teacher values and responds to favorably in terms of written products. Children quickly come to understand what teachers want, and then create products that they think their teachers want to see (DeFord, 1981; DeFord & Harste, 1982). The school setting, because it reflects teachers' assumptions about what writing is, often has a profound impact on children's writing and on children's understanding of writing.

The importance of teachers' assumptions about literacy is illustrated clearly in the reports of face-to-face interactions, both between peers and between teachers and students, in classrooms where writing is viewed as composing and crafting rather than as transcribing. The portraits presented by Calkins (1983) and Graves (1983, 1984) of children as thinkers who reflect upon and make substantive changes in their drafts are portraits painted within the contexts of classrooms organized upon the beliefs that writing is a craft, that people learn from each other, and that writers need to interact with each other in order to develop their abilities. In studying classrooms where such assumptions were put into practice, Calkins and Graves documented that children learned to share their writing with each other, and to exchange comments, questions, and suggestions with their peers. In addition, Calkins and Graves found that teachers met with students for individual conferences, so that writers had another individual audience. A conference provided the chance for further discussion of the creation of a text. Thus, the work of crafting and revising came out of a social context that relied upon sharing and interacting as a major motivation for reflecting upon one's work.

In other classrooms, investigators have discovered that children, even without the teacher's formal organization of such a procedure, will talk with each other as they work on a piece, requesting help on conventions such as spelling, and seeking comments and advice on the substance of a piece. They may also collaborate on a piece especially if they are using a computer. In classrooms that allow and/or encourage student talk and cooperation, then, children serve as co-authors, audiences, and teachers for each other (Genishi & Dyson, 1984; Piazza, 1987; Lamme & Childers, 1983).

Other researchers, examining their own and others' teaching through case studies, have demonstrated the importance of the teacher's nurturance of a setting for writing that includes a view of the relationship of writing to learning school content. These studies have examined the use of journals and learning logs as ways of reflecting on reading and other experiences in school (Atwell, 1987; Fulwiler, 1987), and they have documented teachers' use of writing as a to deal with content in varied disciplines (Atwell, 1987; Hansen, Newkirk and Graves, 1985; Perl &Wilson, 1986).

The Cultural Perspective on Native Language Writing

In addition to being members of a family unit, children are raised as members of a cultural group. Just as there are variations among cultural groups in how talk is viewed, so, too, do cultures vary in their views of writing. The educational anthropologist's perspective is that it is instructive to know how different cultures view writing and how writing functions for various groups, particularly if the schools view writing and its functions differently from the way communities do.

The United States is a culturally diverse nation. In the last ten years, several investigators in various parts of the United States have asked questions about the place of writing within the lives of adults in particular communities. These anthropological investigations have resulted in contrasting pictures of, among other phenomena, the uses and types of writing. The term *use* considers or focuses on the reasons that something is written. For example, a letter can be written for a social purpose such as maintaining a friendship, but a letter can also be written to lodge a complaint about shoddy service or merchandise or to request information. The term *type* refers to the kind of text created. For example, a list, a note, a letter, a poem, a sign, a report, or a check. Findings from three studies carried out in geographically and culturally distinct communities will illustrate these points.

The studies are those of Heath (1983), Taylor (1983), and Taylor and Dorsey-Gaines (1988). Heath compared and contrasted language learning and use, including writing, among three distinct cultural groups living in the same small-town environment of the Piedmont Carolinas in the southeastern United States. Heath labeled the three groups as *Trackton*, a black working-class community, *Roadville*, a white working-class community, and *Townspeople*, a community of black and white residents who considered themselves the mainstream middle-class residents of the Piedmont Carolinas area. Initially, Taylor investigated literacy in white, middle-class families living within a fifty-mile radius of New York City. Later, Taylor and Dorsey-Gaines (1988) studied reading and writing among black families living in the inner city of a major northeastern metropolitan area.

Some uses were common to the adults in all the communities. They all used writing as substitutions for oral messages, as memory aids, as social contacts, and for personal record-keeping. Adults wrote lists and notes; they signed cards and checks; and they wrote out envelopes and order forms. On the other hand, not all of the adults used writing as a way of summarizing discussions and decisions, explaining ideas, deliberating on happenings to increase self-understanding, or creating texts for the purpose of self-expression. In *Roadville* and *Trackton*, for example, children did not see adults writing reports, summaries, papers, journals, stories or poems, while children in *Townspeople* and urban communities did see adults writing these types of texts. Heath has noted that since schools tend to value and promote the latter kinds of writing, children who experience such uses of writing early in their development may be at an advantage in terms of meeting the schools' expectations.

Heath also discovered cultural differences in children's understanding of what constitutes a story. For the *Roadville* children, a story had to be a true happening and did not contain dialogue. For the *Trackton* children, stories were creatively embellished fantasies with dialogues. Heath demonstrated that these understandings of story, both of which were different from teachers' understandings and expectations, had an effect on the kinds of stories children created in school. The *Roadville* children encountered difficulties in responding to teacher requests to make up stories that were imaginative and creative. The *Trackton* children had trouble responding to requests for factual retellings of text material. For both groups of children, their style of creating stories came into conflict with teachers' assumptions about what they would create.

These researchers and others have demonstrated that children growing up in different communities will have varying models both of the content of writing and of the forms or structures that may be used in writing. Children growing up in culturally varied communities will come to understand writing according to community perspectives on what writing is, what writing does, and how writing applies to daily life. As Heath has shown, these varying views take on particular importance when children's writing is considered within the context of the school. In some cases, a community's uses and types of writing parallel closely to that which is valued in school. In other cases, writing in the community and writing in the school differ greatly. Differences may result in misunderstandings and negative perceptions of student abilities, particularly if teachers are not sensitive to cultural differences with regard to writing.

Summary

The research just cited leads to the following conclusions about children's native language writing development.

1) Just as they make sense of spoken language, children make sense of written language. They determine how to construct their own meanings in writing. This process frequently begins long before children begin formal schooling.

2) While they are still learning to talk, children also begin to figure out written language, making and testing hypotheses about the way that written language is structured and used. They create texts based on their hypotheses. As their hypotheses change, so do their surface texts. But, children's intentions from their first efforts are to create meaning. Children are in control of the process.

3) Social factors such as home, the local community, and the print environment surrounding the children play an important part in children's developing understanding of writing, what writing is, what purposes it serves, and how people write and become writers.

4) The school is another important context for writing, and teachers play a critical role in children's writing development. The beliefs and assumptions that teachers hold about writing have an effect on whether children come to see themselves as practitioners of the writer's craft.

5) Cultural factors also play an important role in how children view writing and its function in life.

Given these general conclusions about writing development in a native language setting, the rest of this chapter will use the Piazza framework as a vehicle for summarizing what is known about ESL children's writing. This will provide a comparative view of children's writing in a native language and in a second language.

The Cognitive Perspective on ESL Writing

The first framework used to examine ESL children's writing will be the cognitive one. The first thing that becomes overwhelmingly clear when reviewing the research conducted with ESL children is that, despite the fact that they are lumped together as "second language writers," the children are individuals who come to the second language setting with widely varying native languages, with different cultural backgrounds, and with unique life and schooling experiences. In the same class there may be children from as many as fourteen language groups, some of whom may not have been to school in their home countries, having spent most of their school years in refugee camps (Hudelson, 1988a; Kreeft, Shuy, Staton, Reed, & Morroy, 1984; Urzua, 1986). Some children may have been traumatized during their escapes from war-torn countries (Urzua, 1987b); others may have followed their parents as they migrated, for economic reasons, to and from their home-lands (Samway, 1987b). Some children's previous schooling may have been very different from the kind of schooling they are now receiving (Kreeft et al., 1984). In some cases, the expectations of a previous classroom experience may influence the child's behavior in the new class setting (Hudelson, in press).

Children also come to school, even if they are from the same language group, with unique personalities and varying social styles that may contribute to differences in the ways that they approach tasks and in their willingness to write (Hudelson, in press; Kitagawa, in press). In addition, children come to the second language classroom with varying English ability and with their own unique styles as language learners (Fillmore, 1983; Strong, 1983). Even when learners have been in English language classrooms for the same amount of time, they vary tremendously in how much English they have acquired (Fillmore, 1976). Some learners are more willing than others to take the risks involved in creating meaning through writing (Hudelson, in press). Some will experiment with language while others prefer to use familiar patterns for extended periods of time (Kreeft et al., 1984). ESL writers develop at their own pace; they control the process.

Investigations have shown that, if given the opportunity and encouragement, ESL learners without native-like control of English will work to create meaning in written form, and will make and test out varied hypotheses about how English is written, using whatever linguistic resources are available to them at a particular time. The written products of ESL children look very much like those of young native speakers learning to write English, exhibiting such features as unconventional invented spellings and letter forms, unconventional segmentation and punctuation, and the use of drawing as well as writing to express ideas. The spellings may have their origin in the child's native language orthography, the child's growing understanding of English orthography, the child's unique or community pronunciation of certain words, or in the child's attention to phonetic cues. In addition, the products will reflect the learner's knowledge of the syntactic and semantic systems of English, which may be quite different from the native speaker's knowledge.

Early Second Language Writing

Some examples of children's work should illustrate these points. In the first examples, one kindergarten learner, a native speaker of Spanish (but with no literacy experiences in his native language) has, on two different days, created two crayon drawings. On one he has written *DSLR2D2*. On the other he has noted *DSMANLTDBNQ*. He reads these as *This the R2D2* and *This man stole the bank*. The student has used what he knows about consonants in English and about the spelling of a CVC (consonant-vowel-consonant) word, as well as real world knowledge about *Star Wars* and a local bank robbery, to create his texts. His own pronunciation of *this* as *dis* influences his spelling, as does his pronunciation of *stole* as *stolt*. At this point, his segmentation is also unconventional. He writes, as he talks, in a continuous stream. But he is writing.

Below are three entries from the daily journal of an older child, Betty. When she wrote these entries, Betty was enrolled in a fifth grade classroom in the United States. She had come from Taiwan just before the start of the school year. This was her first experience in an English-medium school, but she had been to school in her own country.

October 7: My name is Betty. My mother name is Jenny. My

father name is Frank. My brother name is Kelvin. My sister name is Daphne. This is my famil.

December 19: Today we go to computer class, I am happy. Yesterday no go to computer class. Today Chinese teacher test we clock minute, hour etc. I like flowers, I want I have one geran.

April 9: It is very special story, please believe me that is truth. When I am first grade one day's afternoon my brother eat one candy I don't know why he laugh they the candy caught in the throat let his face tur to white the mouth ture to black. he fell down and rolled over and over, he is so scared he dead he start call "mom, mom" I saw this is not right.

In Betty's writing in October, she uses a pattern that she knows, repeating it to enable her to create a text to share with her teacher. By December, she knows more English and is willing to venture beyond a safe pattern to experiment with English. Her April entry reveals a child willing to take risks to share something of great importance to her, and a child who demonstrates an awareness that a special introduction may assure her reader's close attention.

Drawing and Writing

Drawing and talking also figure in the writing efforts of second language learners, but individuals vary in how they make use of these other forms of symbolization. Bartelo (1984) examined the drawing and writing of twin six-year-old, first grade ESL learners. As native speakers of Polish (but not literate in their native language) who had been in the United States for about a year, they received English tutoring from the school reading specialist, who shared books and then encouraged the children to write and to draw. Bartelo analyzed the children's drawing and writing. She found that both children made use of drawing but that Sam used drawing more extensively than Susie. Sam always drew before writing, while Susie usually wrote first and then produced a drawing. On half the occasions, Sam's drawing formed the totality of the text he produced. Sam generally added an oral commentary to his drawing; his story could be derived from the combination of his talk and drawing. He often demurred when it came to writing, saying that he did not know how to write. When he did write, Sam copied a sentence from a book or labeled his pictures.

In contrast, Susie's drawings were less complete and complex than Sam's. Susie's written messages carried more meaning than did her drawings. Susie generally wrote at least one sentence and often several sentences about her topic. The talk that accompanied her drawing was not nearly as extensive as Sam's. Bartelo concluded that while both children made use of drawing and talking (to themselves and to the adult) as a way of thinking aloud, Sam made more use of these forms than Susie.

Sam and Susie resemble the second grade beginning-level ESL children that Hudelson studied (in press). One child was comfortable and willing to draw and converse during drawing (although much of the conversing occurred in Spanish, not English) but was unsure of himself and unwilling to write much. The other child was more willing to write, but still preceded writing with drawing and talking.

These examples substantiate that, as with learning to talk, ESL children learning to write are active as language learners. Even beginning ESL children who are not literate in a native language figure out how written English functions, how it should look, and how to use it for their own ends. ESL children, as native speakers, are problem-solvers and hypothesis-generators and testers when it comes to written language. From their writing, it is possible to make inferences about their thinking: how they figure out what to do, how they resolve their problems, and how they create meaning by juggling information and orchestrating the language systems.

The Social Perspective on ESL Writing

Since many ESL learners develop as users of English to a large extent within the context of the school, it is particularly important to examine the school as a social setting for writing and to consider how the social setting may influence the students' perception of writing and its functions and uses. It is also important to study the face-to-face interactions that are a part of writing instruction and the effects of these interactions on the writers.

Investigations carried out in ESL classrooms have indicated that teachers' views of writing have a significant impact on students' ideas of what writing is, and consequently, on students' productions. An illustration of this is the case study of a combined first-second grade class carried out by Peyton (1988). Peyton analyzed the classroom context that influenced a group of beginning-level ESL students with no previous experiences with writing to view themselves as writers and, therefore, to act as writers. Peyton characterized the classroom as a *whole language* classroom filled with meaningful print, including children's books, posters, nursery rhymes, bulletin boards, and so on. The teacher used natural, whole examples of text daily as she read stories and nursery rhymes to children, believing that exposure to *whole language* (rather than to isolated reading skill exercises) would facilitate both the children's construction of meaning from print (reading) and their own construction of text (writing).

The teacher also believed that the children would learn to write by writing, and she modeled writing for the children as a way of demonstrating her processes of thinking about what to write, choosing a topic, and writing. After the teacher modeled writing, she encouraged the children to draw and write as they were able, and she used dialogue journals daily in the class. Dialogue journals are written conversations between two people, in this case between teacher and student. In a dialogue journal, students write to the teacher about whatever they wish. Students turn in their journals, and the teacher reads and responds in writing to the journal entry. The students then read the teacher's response and continue the dialogue. The children in Peyton's study received a considerable amount of time each day to write in their journals, and the teacher called on each child daily to read his or her journal to the teacher, who then wrote a response. Initially some of the children wrote through drawing but quickly they began to add writing to what they were creating. Often the earliest writing took the form of copied words (copied from name tags, books, posters, and so on), but eventually students gained the confidence to create original messages not tied directly to the immediate context.

As the children became comfortable with journal writing, the teacher challenged them to write more and to write with more variety. The teacher also expanded the kinds of writing experiences she offered to the children, adding book journals in which children wrote personal responses to books they read, science journals in which students recorded observations of a plant's growth, and group-written original stories. The teacher believed that these experiences with reading and writing would result in the children becoming readers and writers. And this is precisely what happened. The children gradually became readers and writers of English. The teacher's beliefs about reading and writing led her to set up a certain kind of environment for the children. In addition, she responded to the children's intentions to read and write with the acknowledgment that they were reading and writing. Her creation of a print-rich environment with a variety of literacy activities, the time she allowed for written expression, and her face-to-face interactions with children had a direct effect on her students. The children came to see writing as a natural and important way to communicate a message. They came to see themselves as writers.

Another way of examining the influence of teachers' views of writing is to contrast different teachers and the varying expectations they have for the same ESL learners. In carrying out case studies of primary school ESL children, for example, Hudelson (in press) contrasted children's experiences in their regular classrooms with their experiences with an ESL tutor. Hudelson found that the classroom teacher viewed writing as something that had to be done correctly, that knowledge of spelling and other conventions had to be in place before the independent creation of text should be encouraged or even allowed, and that it was not appropriate to ask children who were still learning to speak English to write in that language. Therefore, the classroom writing that the children did consisted of copying word lists and sentences from the blackboard, filling in the blanks in sentences, and using spelling words to write sentences.

In contrast, the children's ESL tutor viewed writing as the construction of meaning, as the creation of one's messages using whatever language resources one had available at the time. As a result, the tutor encouraged the children to create meaning on topics of their own interest, urging them to see writing as something in process rather than as a finished product that had to be perfect. These diverging teachers' views caused conflict for the children. At the start of the ESL tutoring sessions, children adopted the classroom teacher's view of writing. The children produced remembered versions of textbook exercises, work lists, and sentences using known words. Gradually, theycame to view writing differently and to risk creating their own meanings.

Thus, the teacher's underlying assumptions about how writing is accomplished, why writing is done, and who writing is for may also influence what children produce and the view that they have of themselves as writers. In a study of writing in a bilingual program, Edelsky (1986a, in press-a) documented aspects of the Spanish and ESL writing of Mexican-American children in a bilingual program in Arizona. This program was unlike many others in that the teachers did believe in providing substantial time for writing daily, and they did encourage the children to write in both Spanish and English.

The teachers' understanding of the writing process was limited. They did not understand the idea of writing as a craft, so they did not ask children to share their pieces, to talk with others about what they were doing, to make substantive changes in their pieces, or to revise their pieces to be shared in a final form with others. They did not understand the importance of audience and personal purpose. The children wrote single drafts of pieces in response to an assignment from the teacher. The papers were deposited in writing folders so that the teacher could verify that the assignment had been accomplished. The vast majority of writing in these classrooms was done to satisfy the requirements of the teacher as controller of the class, assignment giver, and evaluator. The teacher, rather than the children, owned the pieces. Edelsky found that the quality of the assigned pieces was not as good as the quality of the few pieces she discovered children had done on their own without an assignment.

Similarly, Hudelson (1986) found that the personal involvement of the writer with the piece had an effect on the quality of the writing. In comparing pieces assigned by the teacher to those initiated by the children, Hudelson found that the unassigned pieces (stories) that the children wrote independently were better written than pieces assigned by the teacher: better in terms of a well-developed story line and of the author's voice or personal involvement with the story.

There was a qualitative difference in work controlled by the children themselves in contrast to work controlled by the teacher. Edelsky (in press-a) has distinguished between *authentic writing* and *writing simulations*, characterizing much of the assigned writing that goes on in school as *writing simulations*.

Watkins-Goffman (1987) also found that student perceptions of the purposes for writing (the writing task) have an effect on the writing they produce. Working with a group of sixth grade ESL learners, Watkins-Goffman found that the children were able to write in a self-expressive way when they perceived that they were writing to a real audience and when they had a stake in the writing, when the writing was purposeful for them. Halsell (1986) noted that young ESL learners who were reluctant to write produced more and better quality writing when they wrote letters to each other and to their teachers utilizing a class mailbox system. Having an authentic audience and purpose made a difference to them.

Dialogue Journals

Kreeft et al. (1984) conducted an examination of the use of dialogue journals with ESL students. Multiple analyses were undertaken using data collected in a sixth grade classroom in Los Angeles, California. The teacher, Leslie Reed, has used dialogue journals for many years, with both native and non-native speakers of English. The data were examined from a variety of perspectives: function of the journals within the framework of the overall classroom; strategies the teacher employed both to promote student participation and to support student effort; patterns of teacher's questions; language input provided by the teacher; language functions used by the teacher and students; use of selected English grammatical morphemes in the journals; and changes in student writing over time, with focus on morpheme use.

For the purposes of this discussion, an important conclusion was that underlying the use of the journals were many assumptions that the teacher held about teaching and learning. These assumptions became explicit as Mrs. Reed participated in the examination of her own teaching with special reference to the dialogue journals. The teacher valued and believed in the journals as a way of getting to know her students, as a way of finding out about her own instruction and about her students' comprehension, as a way of responding to her students individually, as a way for students to express themselves, and as a private channel for honest communication. The teacher encouraged the students to write what they wanted. She put the students in charge of the topics and direction of the journal writing. Students and teacher had equal authority and control (Reed, 1984). The teacher's assumptions about the journals influenced all the students to use the journals for significant communication with the teacher and to use the journals for a variety of functions: reporting on their lives, reporting on school occurrences, sharing what they did and did not understand about school, making complaints, asking questions, and so on (Shuy, 1982).

In regard to the ESL students in particular, Reed discovered that she had assumed that the second language learners would be able to communicate with her in written form, no matter what their length of time in United States schools or their fluency in English. She assumed that the ESL students would use the journals in many of the same ways that the native speakers did, even though they did not have the control over English that the native speakers had. She assumed that the journal experience would be good for the ESL students, in terms of their efforts to communicate, and good for her, in terms of her coming to understand them and their special needs (Reed, 1984). And indeed, the ESL learners did write to Mrs. Reed; they did use the journals for many varied functions, the variety of which was tied to their English as a second language abilities (Shuy, 1984); and they did increase their fluency and control of English over time (Kreeft, 1984). Rather than assuming that ESL learners couldn't write, Reed assumed that they could. This assumption, this faith in the power of the journals and in the ESL students as learners, had a strong effect on their journal production.

Another kind of analysis of the dialogue journals has special relevance for ESL teaching. Staton (1984) found that Mrs. Reed tailored the complexity of her responses to what each reader could understand and answer. Her responses to the more beginning ESL students were shorter and syntactically more simple. She wrote more often in the present tense and used more content words (nouns, verbs, adverbs, adjectives, pronouns) than function words (auxiliary verbs, prepositions, conjunctions, and articles). In terms of interacting features, Mrs. Reed overtly marked the topic she was writing about so that the reader would understand. Often she broke down her initial statements about the topic into two sentences, again to assist comprehension. She asked questions to encourage the learners to respond, using more yes-no questions for her less proficient students. Frequently, she repeated a phrase or sentence the learner had written, as a means of confirming her understanding. In terms of conversational features, the teacher used a wide variety of functions; she made her comments relevant to the other writer's topics; she limited her topics to events or experiences that had occurred during the day in the classroom; and she wrote appoximately the same amount that the students had written, so that they would be able to read and then take a turn at writing.

Staton concluded that Mrs. Reed did what has already been noted for caretaker talk in native language acquisition and teacher talk in second language settings. She tailored her input to the needs and abilities of the learners. She provided the comprehensible input that they needed (Krashen, 1982). She did this in a natural way, unconsciously adapting her language. She herself did not focus on the linguistic forms or on interactive or conversational features. She was concerned about com-municating clearly, about carrying out her part in a conversation, and about facilitating the reader's participation in the written conversation. To do this, she adapted her written language, and she served as an effective language teacher.

Lindfors (1988a, 1988b) used dialogue journals with Zulu students who were ESL learners and found student response similar to that noted in the Kreeft et al. study. Although their language classes were mechanistic, drill-focused, and not communicative in nature, the young people with whom Lindfors dialogued quickly adopted her perspective about the journal writing, quickly came to believe that the journals were to be used for genuine communication about topics of interest to them, and quickly became sharers, question askers, and communicators with Lindfors.

Writing Workshop

A final aspect of writing as social activity that is being studied with ESL students is the face-to-face interactions that occur during writing time, specifically during adaptations of what Calkins (1986) terms the *writing workshop*. In writing workshops, writers create drafts of pieces from self-chosen topics. As they work, they may share a draft or drafts of some of their writing with both the teacher and other children. Sharing of work in progress invites comments and questions from the listeners/readers, and provides input that the writer may use to make substantive changes in the text. Usually in writing workshop classrooms, some of the pieces that children create go through the phases of revision for content and final editing for form before they are *published*. In this context *published* means being put into a format that allows the piece to be shared easily and permanently in the shape of a recopied piece or one that has been typed in book form with illustrations added to it.

Calkins characterizes the workshop environment as "creating a gracious, beautiful setting conducive to craftsmanship" (1986, p.214). While most of the early work done with writing workshops was carried out with native speakers of English (Calkins, 1983; Graves, 1983), Calkins also used writing workshop strategies with bilingual children in New York (Calkins, 1986), and the idea has been advocated for several years by those working in bilingual and second language settings (Allen, 1986; Edelsky, 1982; Hudelson, 1984; Rigg & Enright, 1986; Urzua, 1987b).

Recent investigations of children working in such settings have demonstrated that ESL children are able to create drafts, share them with others, make substantive changes in content based on others' comments, and serve as the listeners and critics of others' work. For example, in an examination of ten- and eleven-year-old children involved in a pullout ESL program that included writing activities, Urzua (1987b) found that the children became quite involved in sharing drafts of stories they wrote outside class, and that both teachers and students responded to the content of the writers' efforts. The teacher first demonstrated the ways in which a listener/reader might respond to a writer's draft. The children soon became adept at doing this.

In studying the children's written drafts that resulted from group sharing and conferencing, Urzua concluded that the writers' work developed in three ways. First, the writers developed a sense of audience. They frequently made substantive changes in their pieces as a result of comments made by others. Second, the writers were able to give their writing a personal voice. Third, the writers became more aware of the power of language. They became more aware that they could manipulate the language, that they could rearrange elements and make substitutions, deletions, and additions. Over time, their repertoires of possibilities increased. The children that Urzua studied had done no writing in ESL classes prior to these experiences and did almost no writing in their regular classrooms. In this particular setting they were able to respond to each other, and they did make substantive improvements in their writing.

Samway (1987b) also investigated what happened when ESL learners participated in writing workshop activities. Working with an ESL teacher in a pullout setting, Samway documented the teacher's work with two groups of students, one a group of second and third graders and the other of fourth and sixth graders. The teacher devoted her ESL classes to literature and writing experiences, suggesting writing topics for the children based on something they had read, but not requiring that the children write on the assigned topic. The teacher also spent time in every class period on individual student-teacher and peer group-teacher conferences. Students shared a draft of their work, and then received questions and suggestions from both the peers and the teacher. Samway was interested in finding out how the students reacted to this classroom, if they did any revising, what kinds of revising they did, and if the sharing and conferencing influenced the learners to make revisions in their work.

Samway observed the children making revisions at a variety of levels. She divided these revisions into three categories: *minimal*, *marked*, and *major*. She defined *minimal* as adding, deleting, or substituting words, phrases, or clauses that didn't change the substance of the piece (revisions at the sentence level or below); changes in punctuation or spelling, recopying; and/or adding a picture. *Marked* revisions were those involving a greater revising of the overall story but revising within the initial boundaries of the story. *Major* revisions involved the writer in creating radically different and new content from what had been written originally.

When she looked at both age levels of children, Samway found that in both groups all three kinds of revisions occurred, but that the techniques used varied according to the individual learner. She did find that *minor* revisions occurred more frequently than *major* or *marked* revisions and that the older children were more likely to make *major* or *marked* revisions than the younger writers. She also found that most of the *minor* revisions focused on changes in words, phrases, or clauses. Very little attention was paid to such mechanics as handwriting, spelling, punctuation, and capitalization, a fact she attributed to the teacher's consistent concern for content rather than form. Samway characterized some of the writers at both age levels as more confident and experienced than others. She found that these writers were more likely to make numerous revisions and revisions that were *major* or *marked*. The less confident writers were more reluctant to make changes in what had been written.

When she looked at the relationship between sharing, conferencing, and revising, Samway found that conferencing influenced revising. More than half of the revisions that she documented were traceable to conferences on a draft a child had written. Samway also discovered that almost half of the pieces that the children wrote, shared, and discussed did not necessarily result in revision. If the children did not choose to revise a piece, they were not required to do so by the teacher.

Samway was also interested in finding out if the revisions improved the quality of the pieces. To do this, she asked teachers to conduct holistic ratings of drafts of the children's pieces. The teachers rated the quality of 50 percent of the revised pieces higher than the original efforts. Twenty-seven percent of the first and second draft pieces were not rated differently, and 23 percent of the second drafts were rated not as good quality as the first drafts. Samway also presented evidence that ESL learners were able to take into account the comments of others on their work. They were also able to react intelligently to work shared with them.

In contrast to work carried out in pullout ESL classes, Gomez (1985) examined the writing workshop carried out in her own sixth grade room, populated by ESL children who were native speakers of Chinese. Gomez spent an hour a day in the writing workshop, working with her children. She assisted them in selecting their own topics, writing drafts of stories, sharing their drafts, participating in writing conferences, and finally editing their pieces. Initially she found that her students were reluctant to share their writing in whole-class conferences. When she switched to peer conferences with two or three children, the children participated much more readily. Using audiotapes and drafts of the children's stories, Gomez discovered that in peer conferences the listeners/readers responded to stories in several different ways. Sometimes their comments focused on details of the story, and they generally requested further information from the writer. Sometimes the listener/reader did not understand part of the story and asked for clarification. At other times, the listener/reader commented on how the story made him or her feel, so that the focus was on an affective aspect of the story. Gomez interpreted these comments as dealing with the content of the piece. The listeners/readers also made comments on the form of the writing. These comments took the form either of remarks about grammatical constructions, or suggestions for changes in spelling, punctuation, and the like.

Gomez also examined what the writers did with these comments. While not all writers acted upon comments from the conferences, Gomez found multiple instances of changes in the writers' pieces resulting directly from their work with another student. While Gomez noted that initially her students were concerned about spelling words in their stories and while initially they had trouble knowing what to do in conferences (a function of never having participated in this kind of activity before), after a short while they were able to participate fully.

The research evidence accumulated so far suggests that the classroom context is critical to the way that second language writers view themselves and the writing process. An environment that encourages ESL students to see writing as a craft to be worked at is an appropriate one for nurturing the developing writing abilities of second language learners.

The Cultural Perspective on ESL Writing

Less research has been done on definitions and functions of writing as a cultural activity in different language communities, and on the implications of cultural differences for learning to write in

English as a second language, than has been done on individual and social aspects of second language writing. Certainly, the work of some educational anthropologists would suggest that discrepancy between the way a particular cultural group views writing or sees the uses or purposes of writing and the way the school views writing may create problems for children in school (Heath, 1983). In many Native American communities, for example, traditions are passed from generation to generation through oral tradition rather than through writing. Writing serves very few purposes in these communitites and may even be viewed as an activity that is counter to the cultural values they are trying to preserve. Children may not see adults engaged in writing (Irvine & Spolsky, 1980; Philips, 1983). All of this may have an effect on how children view writing in school and on whether they will see themselves as writers (Edelsky & Hudelson, 1987).

It would be a mistake, however, to assume that cultural conflicts about literacy issues will always occur when a linguistically and culturally different community comes into contact with the mainstream values of the school. In West Philadelphia, for example, Sino-Vietnamese children in the public schools have made remarkable strides in acquiring school literacy. The children are part of a culture that has one of the world's oldest literacy traditions. In their homes, children see their parents reading letters from and writing letters to their relatives. These activities are valued by the community. In addition, the children's parents place a high value on their children becoming competent readers and writers of English. Frequently, the children help their parents by reading and interpreting English-language documents, by filling out forms, and by writing letters and notes for them in English. In schools, therefore, children work hard to become good readers and writers, attempting to write correctly and neatly, and often choosing to write about their perceptions of the importance of becoming literate in English (Schiefflen & Cochran-Smith, 1984).

It would also be a mistake to assume that because communities have limited access to and uses for literacy, they do not value literacy for their children. In work done in a Mexican immigrant community in southern California, Delgado-Gaitan (1987) has documented community-wide parental expectations and hopes for their children, and parental valuing of literacy, despite limited adult literacy. In this community, parents placed a high value on schooling as a means of pursuing economic rewards in U.S. society. Many Spanish-speaking parents in this community even attended night school ESL classes in order to help their children with their school reading and writing assignments. One cannot assume that because certain groups have limited uses for writing and reading for themselves that they will accept these same realities for their children.

Summary

The following statements may be made to summarize the review of research on ESL children's writing:

1) ESL learners, while they are still learning English, can write; they can create their own meanings.

2) Texts produced by ESL writers contain many of the same features of writing produced by native speakers. These features demonstrate that the writers are making predictions about how the written language works, and they are testing and revising their ideas. Text features change over time, reflecting the writer's changes and growth.

3) While still learning, ESL writers can respond to the works of others and can use responses to their own works to make substantive changes in their creations. ESL learners can engage in writing as a craft, and their understanding of the writer's craft changes over time.

4) There are significant individual differences in how children approach writing and in how they come to see themselves as writers.

5) The classroom environment, including teachers' assumptions about writing, have a significant impact on children's understandings of writing and on the kind and quality of writing they produce.

6) Culture may also have an effect on how writers view writing, the functions or purposes for writing, and themselves as writers.

2

The Place of Native Language Writing in ESL Writing Development

All ESL learners have at least one thing in common: they are native speakers of another language. For many learners, their native language is one in which they are much more fluent than in their second language, and one that they can use for a wide variety of purposes and functions, including demonstrating what they know. In addition, in many cases, learners are literate in their native language. Given this reality, second language educators frequently ask: What is the role of the native language in second language instruction? With reference to children the question is frequently phrased: What role should the native language and native language instruction play in the ESL child's education, particularly with regard to second language literacy development and achievement?

One of the responses has been to make use of the children's native language to teach them. In bilingual education programs, non-English-speaking children learn through the medium of their own languages as well as through English (Crawford, 1987). In terms of the composition focus of this volume, bilingual instruction often has meant teaching non-English-speaking children to read and to write in their native language, often before introducing reading and writing formally in English (see Edelsky, 1986 and Flores, et al., 1985 for discussions of how this has been done with an emphasis on writing).

This chapter presents a perspective on how native language literacy, with specific emphasis on native language writing, may benefit

37

second language (English as a second language) writing. The chapter is an attempt to answer questions posed frequently by elementary school language arts and ESL teachers.

Teacher Questions

1) Does teaching writing and reading in a language other than English retard children's English language literacy development?

2) Isn't it more sensible from the point of view of English growth to teach exclusively in English?

3) Isn't it a waste of time to allow children to learn to read and write in their native language when they need to learn to read and to write in English?

The position taken here is that native language literacy is good, both in and of itself, and because of its positive impact on second language development. This impact manifests itself in several different ways.

First, native language writing experiences help learners understand what writing is and what writing can do. Learners develop a sense of how writers work to create meaning and of the various functions of or purposes for writing. For example, in a bilingual program that emphasized native language (Spanish) writing, children wrote in different genres: pen pal letters, journals, personal narratives, stories, letters to adults, and reports (Edelsky, 1986). In these pieces the children used writing for varied purposes: complaining to a friend, asking questions, issuing invitations, reflecting on personal problems, narrating an event of personal importance, and summarizing or explaining the contents of a lesson or a unit of study.

Because of the amount and variety of writing that they did in Spanish, even though criticisms have been made of the writing instruction that was going on (see chapter one in this monograph for a fuller discussion of Edelsky's research), the children in this bilingual program came to understand what writing was and the varied ways that writing could function. They came to see themselves as writers, which influenced them, subsequently, to see themselves also as writers in English as a second language (Hudelson, 1987).

This understanding of what writing is and this sense of themselves as writers became evident in the confidence the learners displayed when they were asked to write in English. The children could write fluently and easily in Spanish; they were successful at writing. At the end of first and second grade, the children who were writing only in Spanish were asked if they thought they could write in English. In nearly all cases, when asked to do so, the children were willing to write in English, even though they had received no formal writing or reading instruction in English, and even though they still preferred to speak Spanish rather than English. Their writing abilities in Spanish gave them confidence that they could write in English. The children did not see writing in English as a problem. Because they could write in their native language, they believed that they could write in English, and they did so (Edelsky, 1986; Hudelson, 1987). In other settings, too, bilingual educators have noted that ESL children who are fluent writers in one language will decide for themselves when they can write in English and will begin to do so without any formal English instruction (Flores et al., 1985; Hudelson, 1984).

In addition to helping learners understand the functions of writing and giving them confidence that they can write, native language writing provides learners with resources to use as they move into English. These tangible resources include the linguistic abilities and strategies that they develop as they acquire native language writing ability. Having learned to create meaning in their native language, they are able to apply their knowledge to experiment with their second language.

One of the hypotheses that children may make is that English is written the same way as the native language. In the following example, a second grader, enrolled in a bilingual program that stresses native language literacy, has written a story in English. This is the first time the child has written in English, and he has never received formal reading or writing instruction in English. Until now, the child has been free to write (and read) in his native language or in English. He has chosen to do his writing and most of his reading in Spanish, although he has read some library books in English. The class has just seen a movie (in English) about a dragon who is very friendly but sad because by breathing fire he scares people away. The child has decided to write in English, and he produces a tale that is a partial retelling of the story but also includes the child himself as a major actor.

A Child's Story

Ones der was a dragen dat livd in a cav and al av da pipol wer afreyd av him bat all asent afreyd a him pycus all niu jim for a lang taim bat a ditent hant tu tal al av da vilig pipol pycus all av da vilig pypo wr gona go weyfar and all ditent want dat tu japen pycus all wil by sad and al av may frens wil mis mi butma frend da dragen wil by myfrend forever and iv my frend da dregen wil mis ma vileg pypol his by very sad and hil start to dray alat the end.

Once there was a dragon that lived in a cave and all of the people were afraid of him but I wasn't afraid of him because I knew him for a long time but I didn't want to tell all of the village people because all of the village people were gonna go way far and I didn't want that to happen because I will be sad and all of my friends will miss me but my friend the dragon will be my friend forever and if my friend the dragon will miss my village people he'll be very sad and he'll start to cry a lot the end.

A look at the child's first English writing efforts reveals that one of his hypotheses is that English writing goes from left to right. So the child's piece is written from left to right. Another hypothesis is that English uses some of the same orthography as Spanish (the child's native language). Many of the words are spelled using Spanish orthography (*mi, pipol, afreyd, taim*). The writing also demonstrates that the child, who has begun to read on his own in English, uses what he knows about English literacy to give some attention to the English orthographic system. This is evident in his accurate spelling of many words *was, a, far, and, sad, start, the, end, very*. It is also evident in his use of some English letters such as g (*vilig*) which could not be the result of using Spanish and in spelling inventions like those that a native English speaker would make: *livd, forevr, frend*.

Reading and writing in Spanish have given the child the confidence in himself to venture into English reading, and this exposure to English has provided him with resources to help him figure out English. Knowledge of reading and writing also makes the child aware that the same word is usually spelled in the same way. Thus, the child's spelling inventions usually are stable, for example, *pycus, dragen, frend, all, hil, wil,* and so on. In many ways, then, the child uses resources that come not only from Spanish orthography but also from literacy in general (for example, directionality, consistency of spelling) to apply to the task of writing English.

One of the basic tenets of bilingual education is that skills taught in one language transfer to the second language (see Hakuta, 1986; Genesee, 1987 for discussions of this idea). With particular reference to literacy, the point is made that learners learn to read and write only once. Once learners have learned to read and to write, learning transfers to new literacy situations. Edelsky (1982, 1986) uses the term *application* to refer to what happens when learners use their knowledge of their native language in second language situations. By *application,* she means assessing, modifying, and adapting what one knows to fit the demands of a new situation. By using the term *application* rather than *transfer,* Edelsky describes the learner as the active person in charge of the literacy process.

Edelsky (1982, 1986) examined the ways in which children apply knowledge acquired as they become writers in their native language to writing in English as a second language. As the previous example illustrates, she discovered that the young writers used knowledge, hypotheses, and strategies developed in writing Spanish and applied them to the problems of spelling, segmentation, and punctuation in ESL. In addition, they used their ever growing knowledge of written English, gleaned from English texts and environmental print, without having had formal literacy instruction in English. Over time, as the children learned more and more about English, their texts came to include more of the features of the written language.

Edelsky also found that the children she studied used what they had learned in Spanish about broader, more global aspects of writing when they wrote in English. For example, the children learned a format for writing letters when they wrote in Spanish to their pen pals in another school. When they began to write letters in English, they used the same format. In one classroom where the teacher praised long pieces, children who wrote lengthy pieces in Spanish also wrote lengthy pieces in English. Edelsky (1982) referred to this as making use of everything you have to create meaning in English.

Edelsky and others have demonstrated that second language learners are actively engaged in figuring out how the writing system of their second language works, and that they use the system to communicate and express themselves. Learners who already have gone through this problem-solving as they acquired writing ability in their native language have learned how to learn. As they formed hypotheses about L1 (first language) writing, as they tried out and modified their predictions, and as they attended to features of the written system of their native language, they apply that knowledge and those strategies to writing in a second language.

Native language writing gives learners a chance to demonstrate some of what they know in a language that they control. On the basis of research and classroom experience, ESL educators maintain that children can write in ESL before they have complete control over the systems of English (Hudelson, 1984, 1986). Based upon the research cited, this position appears justified.

It is also true that children who are still in the throes of learning English are aware that they have limited control over the language. Therefore, some children are quite reluctant to write in their new language, expressing concern that either they do not know enough English or they do not know how to write in English at all (Bartelo, 1984; Hudelson, in press). Some children may even refuse to write in English because of their insecurities about the new language. Allowing these children to write in their native language, even if the class is labeled ESL, may provide them with a way of expressing themselves and their knowledge and with a mechanism for being a part of classroom activities until they feel confident enough to begin using English.

Kitagawa (in press) reports on just such a situation. Her English-medium sixth grade classroom consisted mostly of Spanish-English bilingual children. When Juan, a refugee from El Salvador, came to her class, he was unwilling to speak English, and he refused to use the language for writing. The children wrote in journals every day, and Kitagawa responded to the journals. Juan was willing to write if he could write in Spanish. Even though her Spanish was very limited, Kitagawa allowed Juan to write in Spanish. She did try to respond in Spanish, but she finally requested that he try to write to her in English, so that she could understand him better. Gradually Juan began to write in English. His teacher's willingness to let him create meaning in Spanish meant that he could participate in the journal activity and gradually, exercising some control, progress to writing English.

But what if the teacher does not know the language of the children? This was the case in two Atlanta classrooms, where second language learners from fourteen different languages learned alongside native speakers of English. In these team-taught fifth grade classrooms, the teachers used journals with their children. Most of the children, even those with very limited English abilities, wrote in English. In January of the school year, a child from Portugal joined the class. Because she was not comfortable writing in English, her teacher allowed her to write in Portuguese, even though the teacher neither spoke nor read Portuguese. After a period of a few weeks, the child began to venture into writing in English.

Later in the school year, a child from Korea entered the fifth grade. By this time the children were writing auto-biographies, and the Korean child created one entirely in Korean. She also illustrated several of her pieces, and the illustrations provided clues to the contents of several of the chapters, for example, playing ball, studying at her Korean school, coming to the United States on an airplane, studying English at her new school, and her trip to Disneyworld. In the chapters about studying English and going to Disneyworld, she even wrote some English words in parentheses in her text, indicating that she was beginning to read English, and she provided an illustration of the letters of the English alphabet, followed by Korean writing. The words *I'm here, what, Garden Hills, Snow White, Fort Bear, Mickey Mouse,* and *I love you,* showed clearly that the child was attending to English and acquiring English literacy while living in a new country. The attention to the English alphabet demonstrated

Write On

that the child was comparing what she already knew (Korean) to something new (English). If this child had not been allowed to write in Korean, she would not have been able to contribute her life story to the class project. And she might not have provided such strong evidence of the process of acquiring written English.

This particular child did not write in English during the rest of the school year. But she did attend summer school, and, at that time (late June) began to participate in the daily journal writing that was part of her summer school class. The two journal entries below, one from June and one from July, suggest the progress she was making in creating meaning through the medium of written English.

A Child's Journal

June 25

Today is Wednesday
My teacher is Mrs. J
Today we play jumprope say the
color ball and drow the my face.
I like to this play.
And my class.
Today is very fun day.

July 10

2 days ago we played pinata.
In the pinata there was candy and
paper. I taked 5 candys.
I meet Mrs. S. She's my
brother's teacher. We leared terrarium.
and yesterday we cooked cakes.
It was black and small.
we used the dried grapes, cake mix,
and apple sauce. very good
yesterday and today we drowed the
monster. It drow the 4 people.
He has many hands, each has 2 fingers,

1 cloth 2 eys, and many foods.
It looks like an octopus.
And with him taked the picture.
Today I say the my picture.
It taked the savannah.

While the claim might be made that this child used her native language as a crutch for a brief period of time, she did begin to take risks with written English after only a few months of experience with the new language. The fact that she could use Korean did not deter her from acquiring English. Rather, it allowed her to show her intellectual capabilities and her individuality while acquiring English. Gradually, she became comfortable enough with English that she was willing to use it to create meaning in writing.

The previous discussion is not to suggest that ESL approaches that do not include native-language exercises are not appropriate for children. Certainly, a major goal of language education in this country is to develop students' ability to use English effectively, and to learn school content through English. And in many situations, it is not possible or sensible, for any number of reasons, to provide native language instruction. This was the case in the Atlanta school, where there were so many different languages represented that it was not possible to provide instruction in a language other than English. It is important to recognize, however, that bilingual schooling that includes native language literacy may make important contributions to second language growth. The native language is a valuable resource for students as they go about the business of learning English, including learning how to write in English. It is also vital to acknowledge, as the Atlanta teachers and Kitagawa did, that the native language is a positive and valuable classroom resource. Even when teachers do not read and write the native languages of the students, allowing students to express themselves in writing in their native language provides a way for teachers to learn something about their students and what they know.

Summary

When second language learners are literate in their native language, these reading and writing abilities may have positive effects on their second language development, especially second language reading and writing. Native language writing ability has positive benefits in terms of second language writing:

1) Learning to write in the native language exposes learners to the functions and purposes of writing, so that learners understand what writing is for.

2) Writing ability in the native language provides second language learners with resources (both linguistic and nonlinguistic) that they can use as they approach second language writing. Second language learners are able to apply the knowledge about writing gained in first language settings to second language settings.

3) Native language writing allows second language learners to demonstrate some of what they know in a language they control. Second language learners are thus able to show their competence rather than their incompetence and to grow in their confidence in themselves as learners. This, in turn, may have positive effects on learners' willingness to risk writing in their new language.

3

Writing Instruction for the Elementary ESL Student: Applications from Research

The research reviewed in chapter one makes the case that writing ability is acquired and developed through meaningful and continued writing. Therefore, writing should be included as an integral part of second language activities in elementary schools. This perspective is not unique to second language settings. Some readers may recognize it as one that has been proposed for native speakers of English as a *whole language* approach to education. Grounding their perspective in the kind of language research that has been reported in this volume, *whole language* advocates assert that literacy learning takes place within the context of reading and writing natural, authentic, and whole texts (Goodman, 1986), rather than through dividing language into bits or subskills and practicing these subskills. *Whole language* educators maintain that learners do not first learn to read and write and then learn school content. Rather, as learners explore topics of interest to them, they naturally engage in reading and writing about these topics. It is through such engagements that literacy develops. Students become readers and writers and learn more about written language and about the power of literacy by carrying out meaningful reading and writing activities. Many second language educators have utilized these principles in their ESL work (Allen, 1986; Edelsky, 1986; Enright & McCloskey, 1985; Rigg & Enright, 1986; Urzua, 1987a).

Given the support for the *whole language* approach, a question arises: How do teachers include writing as a part of the learning experiences of their second language learners? To begin to answer that question, some general suggestions might be made.

Writing as Part of the Learning Experience

1) Make time for writing on a regular basis. Even five to ten minutes daily of diary or dialogue journal writing should help ESL learners begin to understand that they can use writing to express themselves, to create meaning, and to experiment with the written forms of the English language to convey their intentions. Learners acquire writing ability at least partially by writing. ESL learners will not develop as writers if they do not have opportunities to write.

2) Work initially to encourage ESL children's willingness to write, to promote fluency in their writing despite the "errors" made. Writing requires that learners take risks and make mistakes as they test out their hypotheses about how written English works and as they struggle to write what they mean. Perhaps even more than native speakers, ESL learners need to be assured that it is acceptable to make guesses about how to write something, that it is natural to make mistakes, that it is okay to put something down even if it is not exactly what you want to express, that is is better to construct some tentative ideas that can be improved rather than writing nothing at all. Teachers need to take the view that a written draft is work in progress rather than a completed product.

This does not mean that learners should not share what they are writing with others. Nor does it mean that listeners/readers should not respond to what a writer has written by commenting and asking questions, and offering suggestions and criticisms. It does mean that first efforts and fluency should be encouraged. Writers should be helped to see that their efforts are valued, that they will not be satisfied with everything they are writing, and that they will want to make substantive changes.

3) Respond to writing by focusing on the messages that learners are sending, the meanings that they are constructing, rather than on the forms used to create the messages. Primary atten-

tion must be given to what learners are trying to convey with written language, to the purposes for which they are writing, rather than to the manner in which conventional (adult standards) symbols appear.

In talking about native speakers of English, Smith (1982) distinguishes between composing and transcribing, noting that composing is the creative act while transcribing is concerned with the surface features and conventions of the creation. It is his contention that children become writers only as they come to see composing as primary in importance and transcribing as secondary. What he writes about native speakers also holds true for the ESL student.

4) Authenticity of purpose is crucial to ESL writing. Writers need to be engaged in writing for reasons that are real and important to them. Both the quality of writing and the level of the writer's involvement with the task are a reflection of the writer's understanding of what writing is, why people write, and for whom. Learners need varied experiences with writing, experiences that help them understand that they can use writing for self-reflection and for creating meaning that they want to communicate to others. Writers must be given the opportunity to create authentic texts, texts that reflect their intentions as writers.

Create the Atmosphere and Teach Children to Write

The rest of this chapter offers some more specific suggestions about writing instruction for ESL children. These suggestions are based on personal interpretations of research and on successful classroom practice that uses a *whole language* approach.

A fact to remember when setting up a framework for classroom practice is that writing varies. This implies that people write for different purposes, uses, or functions, that people write for different audiences, that people write on different topics.

Think of yourself: What kinds of writing do you do each day — and why do you write? One individual might produce the following: a list of items to be purchased at the drug store, a check to the newspaper carrier to renew a subscription, a letter to a niece about colleges to which she is thinking of applying, notes for a presentation to be given at a meeting the following week, directions to a friend on how to get to a downtown theater to see a play, a letter to an airline requesting usage of frequent flyer mileage reimbursement, a stanza of a funny poem to be given to friends celebrating a wedding anniversary, and a journal entry to record the important events of the day.

Even a cursory glance at this list makes it clear that people write different kinds of pieces (lists, letters, instructions, notes, poems, narratives) for different purposes (to jog one's memory, to meet a financial obligation, to make a request, to present information or an argument, to reflect, and to amuse) to different audiences (self, friends, relatives, colleagues, a company).

Moving from the individual writer to the classroom, several educators have applied the idea of language functions or purposes to frameworks for developing writing abilities in schools. Britton (1970) and his colleagues (Britton et al., 1975) have divided language use in general and writing in particular into three main categories: *expressive writing, poetic writing,* and *transactional writing.* They define expressive writing as writing that reveals the person as an individual, writing that focuses on the individual's feelings, emotions, and ideas. Examples of this kind of writing are diaries, journals, and personal narratives. The audience for this kind of writing is often oneself, but the audience may also be another person.

Poetic writing refers to writing that uses artistic and literary aspects of language in the creation of pieces that belong to particular genres, such as, stories, poems, fables, folktales, jokes, limericks, and songs. The writer intends for the audience to enjoy the piece. The writer is also concerned with using particular literary elements effectively in crafting a piece.

In contrast, transactional writing focuses on writing to get things done. Here the writer is especially concerned with writing clearly for an audience, emphasizing clarity and organization so that the reader will have no doubt as to the author's intended meaning. In transactional writing, the writer is motivated to describe, to explain, to argue a point of view, to address and answer questions, or to summarize. Reports and summaries are typical of the kind of writing called transactional.

Other language educators have proposed different ways of looking at the uses or functions of language and writing. Kinneavy (1971), for example, uses the terms *self-expressive* and *literary* writing in the same way as Britton uses the terms *expressive* and *poetic*. Kinneavy then divides transactional into *informative* and *persuasive*, separating the function of convincing someone of a point of view from that of giving information and explaining. Borrowing from Halliday's list of language functions (1973), Smith (1982) has suggested that there are ten basic ways in which people use language, whether oral or written. Many of Smith's uses relate directly to Britton's categories of expressive, poetic, and transactional writing.

Britton has stated that often the functions of writing are not mutually exclusive. That is, the writer may combine transactional with expressive purposes, or poetic with expressive. Berthoff (1981) also makes this point as she criticizes approaches to teaching writing that polarize poetic and transactional (or expository) writing and suggest that they are completely different from one another, rather than seeing the aspects that they have in common. It is not the aim of this discussion to set up mutually exclusive categories, particularly in terms of teaching. Rather, the categories may be used as a general framework for applying findings from research on children's writing in a second language to classroom practice.

Expressive Writing

Britton has suggested that the first kind of writing to develop is expressive writing, the kind of writing that reveals the individual and focuses on individual experiences, feelings, and emotions. While Newkirk (1984) has argued with Britton's contention about the primacy of expressive writing for the LEP (limited English proficient) students in elementary school, expressive writing may be the most sensible place to start. By beginning with expressive writing, learners will start with something they know: their experiences and their personal feelings. Encouraging expressive writing will allow learners to share themselves. Teachers and peers will come to know the LEP students as people (Kitagawa, in press) and not just as non-native speakers of English.

One way to approach expressive writing is to use diaries or journals with ESL learners, allowing children a few minutes daily to write about personal matters of importance to them. Dialogue journals, even though they take more time than journals that are not conversational in nature, are especially recommended in the second language context.

Peyton (1987, p. 1) defines a dialogue journal:

> a written conversation in which a student and teacher communicate regularly—daily, if possible, or at least two or three times a week. Students may write as much as they choose on any topic and the teacher writes back regularly to each student (each time they write, if possible)—often responding to the student's topics, but also introducing new topics; making comments and offering observations and opinions; requesting and giving clarification; asking and answering questions. The teacher's role is as a participant with the student in an ongoing, written conversation, rather than as an evaluator who corrects or comments on the writing.

Dialogue journals are an especially effective way of moving second language learners into writing (Kreeft et al., 1984). They are also an effective tool in second language acquisition since they provide individualized comprehensible input (Krashen, 1982) in the form of the teacher's responses to each student writer (Staton, 1984). All that is required for a dialogue journal is a set of blank notebooks for students and time set aside for writing. Time may be provided when students come to school in the morning, after lunch, or at the beginning or close of the ESL class (for pullout ESL classes). Still another alternative is to distribute the journals when the students arrive in the morning and allow them to keep their journals all day, so that they may write whenever they have the time and the inclination (Kreeft et al., 1984).

Because much of the published research on dialogue journals has been carried out with students beyond the primary level, teachers working with younger children (kindergarten through third grade) may ask if it is realistic to use dialogue journals with children who are just learning to write. Teachers want to know if they can use journals with children whose reading is difficult to understand and with those children who express much of their meaning through pictures instead of graphic symbols. It is certainly feasible and rewarding to utilize dialogue journals with younger students, but the ways in which the activity is organized may need to be adjusted to the needs and writing abilities of the younger learners.

In a first grade classroom (Flores & Garcia, 1984; Flores et al., 1985), the teacher set aside a brief amount of time each morning for children to write. Early in the year the teacher could not interpret much of what the children wrote. Therefore, as the children completed their writing and drawing, the teacher immediately asked the children to read to her what they had written, at which point she composed a response, and read her response back to each individual child. Then the journals were put away until the next day. This way of managing the dialogue journals allowed the teacher both to acknowledge the children's creation of meaning (even as they helped her by reading what they had written) and to write a meaningful response.

Personal Communication

Peyton observed a first grade teacher using journals in the same way. Peyton has noted that, with this kind of immediate response a sustained conversation about a topic over several days, cannot occur even when the teacher invites comments and asks questions in her responses. This may happen because when the children write in their journals the next day, they have already read what the teacher has written and do not feel a need to read it again. In contrast, if the teacher responds to journals when the learners are not present, the children do not know what she has said/written, and there is both an authentic reason to read the teacher's entry, and perhaps, to respond to the teacher's comments and questions.

In a variation on dialogue journals, Kitagawa (in press) reports responding to her students' journals using the Japanese technique of *akapen*. This technique involves the teacher in considering carefully what the writer has written and then writing statements that reflect understanding of and attention to the details of what the writer has created. Rarely does the teacher ask questions or introduce new topics. The emphasis is on careful reflection on the writer's narration, often by writing in the side margin, responding to whatever strikes the reader as significant or interesting. An example of *akapen* response may help to clarify these points.

Child's entry	**akapen**
...When I was done (fixing tortillas and other ingredients) I put the enchiladas in a plate and had to heat up the sauce cause it was cold. When I turned it on I went to watch tv. I couldn't wait to taste it so I went to the kitchen and put it high and went to the table to waite. When I turned around there was cheese on the ground and everywhere so I thought it was ready. And when I ate them I only ate five because I made five for my big dog and three for my small dog and they were good but I saw the mess and cleaned it up before mom got here	**It is hard to get everything hot at the same time.** **You're impatient at this point. Cheese boiled over, I guess. Your dogs sure appreciate your cooking, but maybe your mom doesn't.**

(Kitagawa, in press)

Some teachers do not have the time or energy to invest in dialogue journals, but they are interested in encouraging self-expressive writing. Another way to do this is to have students write in diaries or journals that are not interactive. It is obviously crucial that students view this as valuable to them, something that allows them to reflect on their own lives. This might be a challenge without the teacher's "conversing." Nevertheless, it is possible to create a classroom environment where students are excited by their journals and diaries and enjoy writing in them, whether they choose to keep them private or to share them with the teacher. The example that follows exemplifies a diary being used by a student to wrestle with her personal problem outside of school. This particular child chose to share her diary with her teacher, who understood the child better after reading her entries.

Diary entry:

My mom is having a baby I hope it is a girl It wood be nice to have to boys and to girls that wood be the same thing I wood like it the house is geting small we don't have no room What to do is hard to do it Mom and Dad what are we going to do I don't no E____ I'am sorry I can help it

It is also possible to have students carry on written journal conversations with each other. In their work with deaf elementary school students, Peyton and Mackinson-Smythe (in press) have demonstrated this possibility. American Sign Language was the native language for these children and English their second language. Pairs of children used a computer network to write to each other. The researchers found that the children were able to initiate and sustain conversations with each other. In paired situations where one child had more fluency in English than the other, the more able child adjusted her input to assist the less fluent child to understand and respond to the conversation. Topics of interest to the learners made up the written conversations, and the children were successful in communicating with each other.

The Writing Workshop in ESL Classes

The other major activity in the area of expressive writing that many people have advocated for second language learners (Edelsky, 1986; Gomez, 1985; Hudelson, 1984, 1986; Samway, 1987b; Samway & Alvarez, 1987; Urzua, 1987b) is called *process writing* or sometimes *writing workshop*, which involves children in the construction of personal narratives. In process writing children generate topics that they would or could write about, topics in which they have interest and expertise. Children then choose a subject and create narratives. Often the teacher models the process of generating topics and beginning a draft by choosing a topic on which he or she is an expert. Then, the teacher begins to write in front of the children. Frequently, too, children interview each other and generate topics in that way (Graves, 1983).

Central to process writing/writing workshop is children's sharing of some of their writing. Sharing is usually done with an audience of peers and teachers who receive the piece (Graves, 1983) and reflect on what they read, comment on the piece, ask questions about parts of what has been written, and offer direction and encouragement to the writer. Children may then use the feedback from their audiences as they make substantive changes in what they have written. Not every piece that a child writes needs to be shared and revised.

As a final step to the writing process, usually some of what a child writes is "published," that is, put into a final form for others to read and enjoy, often with illustrations that the author creates to accompany the story. Before a work is published, editing takes place, with its focus on the conventions of the language. This is when standard spelling, punctuation, and rules for capitalization are observed, and when teachers are able to point out these features of standard written language to the learners. Editing is always done in the context of writing for an authentic audience.

What about Grammar?

Teachers of second language learners frequently ask how much editing should be done and how much emphasis should be given to correcting grammatical "errors" in the final version. No definitive answer will be satisfactory in all cases. In terms of spelling and other mechanical areas, if a draft contains multiple errors, it is better to correct a few of the errors, selecting those problems that have occurred repeatedly (for example, a stable spelling invention such as *frend* for *friend*, or the consistent omission of a capital letter at the beginning of a sentence).

In terms of grammar, second language learners will write using the grammatical structures over which they have control at that given point in time. If learners controlled the standard forms, they would use them correctly. This suggests that the correction of grammatical "errors" should be approached with care. Again, it may make sense to choose one or two features that the learner uses consistently (for example, expressing the singular form of the present tense without the s) and point out the standard written form. It is crucial that teachers remember that pointing out the standard form and asking the learner to copy a piece of writing using the standard form will not necessarily mean that this form will be used in subsequent writing. At least as important as the direct editing of students' writing is the exposure to standard written English from authentic texts. This perspective will be discussed in some detail in the next section of this chapter.

To conclude the discussion of process writing, the emphasis in this approach is on the process of crafting a piece of writing, rather than simply on a finished product. And despite the suggested linearity in this description, the reality is that the process rarely proceeds in such a straightforward fashion. Instead there is a recursiveness, a movement back and forth between drafting and revising, between considering and jotting down topics. Essential to the process is a teacher who demonstrates aspects of the craft of writing, such as brainstorming topics, choosing topics, beginning a draft, sharing an effort, making comments, and using comments to redraft. The teacher sets the tone, encourages children in their efforts, focuses on the children's creation of meaning, and helps them deal with editing.

It could be argued that the narratives created in process writing are not strictly self-expressive, but rather contain elements of poetic or literary writing. Researchers who have examined the kinds of writing that usually come out of writing workshops (whether with native speakers or ESL students) suggest that most often children write personal narratives; they tell stories of events in their own lives (Calkins, 1983; Gomez, 1985; Graves, 1983; Samway, 1987b). Sometimes children move back and forth between fact and fiction, combining elements of both, as does the following example, which begins with the writer's Smurfy doll and then adds elements of fantasy probably inspired by cartoon shows of monsters (Hudelson, 1986).

> One day Smurfy and I went to sleep. I had a sweet dream at first but then it turn into a horrible dream. I was at the park one day when the sky got so dark, it was like midnight. Everyone was pushing and shoveling trying to get home. I

Write On

sat on the bench and Smurfy sat beside me to keep out off everybody's way. It was very quiet and began to blow and howled. It blew so hard that Smurfy flew away and hide behind a tree. Suddenly, the lightning crashed and the thunder roared the the thunder crashed. It was an unfriend roar, it sounded like it was mad at somebody or something. Sudenly, there was a loud noise. I looked around for Smurfy. It was like being blind because I had to use my hands and legs to feel things. The lightning roared at my smurf and flash the light on it, it look as though would burn. The thunder crashed. The lightning and the thunder seem as though as it was give the little smurf power. Smurfy became alive and he was growing and growing. His face, feet and arms were so wierd. It puted out it's arms as it walked toward me. Oh no, my precious Smurfy, it has turn into a horrible horrible monster by the lightning and Thunder! It grab me and flew into the sky. We flew higher and higher. "Somebody stop it," I said. "lightning, thunder, bird, eagle, whatever, just stop this creature!" I said. I stopped a minute and think. "Mother earth, please change this monster back to my smurf!" I yelled. The monster begin to shrink smaller and smaller. I fainted and we both started falling. I held on to my smurf and floated in the sky.

> From *Children and ESL: Integrating perspectives* (p. 44) by P. Rigg & D. S. Enright. Washington, DC: Teachers of English to Speakers of Other Languages. Copyright 1986 by TESOL. Reprinted by permission.

This piece provides evidence that young writers do not limit themselves to writing accounts of things that have happened to them. There is also evidence that as young writers, whether native speakers of English or ESL students, read literature of many forms, their writing will be influenced by their reading, and they will begin to write more like readers (Allen, 1986; Calkins, 1986; Smith, 1982).

Poetic Writing and the Reading/Writing Connection

The idea of writing like a reader is one that moves the discussion to an emphasis on poetic (or literary) writing, writing that puts more emphasis on the formal literary elements that make up a certain genre. Here genre means a specific literary form such as the story, the fable, the tall tale, the rhyme, the limerick, the ballad, and so on. If, for example, children were creating versions of what some might call the classic fairy tale, their stories probably would include the setting, the characters, an initiating event, a conflict, and resolution of the conflict. On the other hand, if children were creating limericks, they would probably be concerned with focusing on a single character. They would probably begin the first line with "There was a _____", and the second with "Who/Whose _____." They would also need to follow the pattern of five lines, with nine syllables in the first, second, and fifth lines, rhyming of the first, second and fifth lines, and six syllables in the third and fourth lines.

Awareness of poetic or literary forms comes through the experience of listening to and reading a variety of genres. In order to write classic fairy stories, children need to have listened to and read such stories. In order to write limericks, children need to have listened to and read limericks. With regard to poetic writing, reading and responding to or reflecting upon literature is vital to being able to write it. This has been termed the reading-writing connection (Calkins, 1986). As children become readers and responders to literature in all its forms, their efforts at crafting pieces are influenced by what professional writers do. When encouraged to write using a process approach, children come to see themselves as real authors who create literary pieces in the same way as familiar authors do. This does not mean that they produce well-constructed stories, poems and the like, automatically and without considerable effort. It does mean that wide reading is crucial to seeing oneself as an author, and to applying literary knowledge to the craft. For this reason, Graves (1983) advocates surrounding children with many kinds of good literature.

Educators working with second language learners have made a

variety of suggestions for using literature with ESL learners. Several of these will be discussed here. The first suggestion is that teachers set aside a time daily for reading books, stories, poems, and so on to children, in effect, a class story time. For second language learners a sensible place to begin story time is with stories and books that are highly predictable. Beginning with a definition of reading as a process in which readers predict their way through texts (Goodman, 1967), sharing materials that are highly predictable will increase readers' abilities to read such texts themselves. Certain kinds of reading materials are more predictable than others (Heald-Taylor, 1987; Rhodes, 1981). In some texts, factors within the texts themselves, such as repetition of language and incident, contribute to predictability. Common fairy tales such as *The Three Little Pigs, Little Red Riding Hood, The Three Bears, Chicken Little,* and *The Little Red Hen* are examples of predictable reading materials. In *The Little Red Hen,* for example, the hen repeatedly carries out tasks by herself while asking over and over, "Who will help me ____ the corn?" And her friends consistently respond, "Not I." These repetitions help the reader predict what the hen and her companions will do and say.

Other stories are predictable in part due to rhythm and rhyme. In the story *May I Bring a Friend?* (deRegniers, 1965), as the main character brings a succession of wild animals to a fancy party, he repeats these lines: "I told the king and the king told the queen that I had a friend I wanted to bring. The queen said to me, 'My dear, my dear. Any friend of yours is welcome here.' " Children's songs such as "Old MacDonald Had a Farm" and " I Know an Old Lady Who Swallowed a Fly" also fall into this category, as do poems such as "This Is the House That Jack Built." Finally, some children's books such as *The Carrot Seed* (Krauss, 1945) and *The Very Hungry Caterpillar* (Carle, 1969) are predictable for readers who can take advantage of real world knowledge in these two cases, of how plants grow and how caterpillars turn into butterflies. Using predictable stories exposes ESL learners to one kind of book talk or poetic language. Then, as children become comfortable with these highly predictable literary forms, increasingly varied and more complex forms of literature should be introduced (see Bird & Alvarez, 1987; Edelsky, in press-c; Flores et al., 1985; Samway & Alvarez, 1987, for examples of the kind of literature being studied by children labeled as limited speakers of English).

Daily storytime should continue, no matter what the grade level, as educators working with ESL intermediate grade children have shown (for example, Hayes & Bahruth, 1985a). Often older children, because they have been labeled as language-deficient, have been subjected to several years of a "reductionist curriculum" (Cazden, 1986) by educators who have assumed that until they have mastered all the subskills of reading, they cannot handle or enjoy literature. In fact, these children need and deserve multiple examples of the world of books and poetic or literary language. As older children listen to stories, they soon begin to read along with the teacher and then to pick up the stories to read themselves. They begin to be "hooked on books" (Hayes, Bahruth & Kessler, 1985b; Samway & Alvarez, 1987; Urzua, 1987a).

Responses to books may come in several forms, including art and drama. Responses also involve children in writing, either group writing of plays or skits based on stories (which would also involve children in rehearsing and performing the play that had been written), or creation of original pieces based on the form or language of something read to them or by them (Piper, 1986). For example, in a fourth grade class populated by second language learners, a teacher read the children Remy Charlip's *Fortunately*. This story deals with a series of events that befall the story's protagonist, each event following the preceding one and beginning with the words *fortunately* or *unfortunately*. The children enjoyed the story and wanted to create their own versions of the story. They chose to use *that's good/that's bad* instead of *fortunately/unfortunately*, and created some stories which they shared with one another. In the one reproduced below, it is clear that the author has understood Charlip's technique and has used it to create a story.

Good or Bad
Hey I just lost my ball
That's bad
No that's good because I found it
again
Oh that's good
No that's bad because I found the

rongh one
That's bad
No that's good because I put
up a sign
saying lost ball pleas find it
That's good
No that's bad because a lot of people
came with balls
That's bad
No that's good because I checked
them all
That's good
No that's bad because they were all
red
That's bad
No that's good because I had it in
my
pocket all the time

In addition, even if children are not imitating the form or language of a particular story, when they understand and become sensitive to story talk and story conventions, they begin to use them in their own writing. As Calkins (1986) notes, they want their own stories to sound like the stories that they are reading. More on this idea will be developed later in the discussion of a literature-based reading program.

From storytime orchestrated by the teacher, teachers may move to provide opportunities for learners to read, independently, material of their own choosing. Some reading educators have labelled this practice *Silent Sustained Reading*. Another term used is *DEAR* time—Drop Everything and Read (Flores et al., 1985). The essence of this practice is that every day, at a particular time of the day, children and teacher read to themselves books or stories that they have chosen. Nothing else may occur at that time. Spending time on an activity like this in class affirms the importance of literature, as opposed to the general daily dose of basal readers and content area texts students must cope with. Often children choose to read on their own a story or book that the teacher has shared in class. Or children may choose another story by the same author or a story or book on a topic of personal interest to them. In some classes, children are able, after DEAR time, to share with each other what they have been reading, which also stimulates later reading selections by class members (Flores et al., 1985).

To repeat, when children move from reading to writing, elements of stories appear in children's writing, and children often create their own stories based on a particular genre that they have been reading (Allen, 1986). Flores et al. (1985) use the following story to illustrate the way in which reading tall tales influenced a child to write her own tall tale. Having read Paul Bunyan and Pecos Bill tales, this child created her own, one in which the elements of a tall tale are certainly evident.

The Tallest Man

Once there was a man that was taller than the biggest building in the world. He could touch the building and the building would fall. When he stood up he was taller than the building. He sometimes would touch the sky. He would sometimes catch a cloud. One day a little kid found him dead. He was dead because he was so old, and the kid cried and cried. He was so dad that that he grew up like him. The kid was the tallest man in the whole world!

> From *Holistic Bilingual Instructional Strategies* (p. 60) B. Flores et al. Phoenix, AZ: Exito, 1985. Copyright by Exito and the authors. Reprinted with permission of the authors.

One reality for ESL learners in elementary schools, especially for intermediate grade students, is that they often do not do well on standardized or criterion referenced tests of language arts and reading. This results in schools viewing them either as unintelligent or as language-deprived, and in instituting remedial programs to "teach them the basics." As a consequence, many children do not see themselves as readers and writers. They think that they are unable to read (Urzua, 1987a). One way to counteract this situation is to use an activity of shared-book experiences, in which older students (intermediate grade students—fourth through sixth graders) choose books to read to younger pupils (Flores, et al., 1985). The older students prepare themselves for this tutoring task by reading many children's books (Edelsky, cited in Alvarez, 1988). This exposes them to the book talk and story grammar of predictable children's books but for an authentic purpose: to share the book with someone else.

One implementation of this shared-book idea occurred at Fair Oaks Elementary School in Redwood City, California, as part of an experimental interactive reading program (Heath, 1986). In this project (Samway & Alvarez, 1987), sixty low-achieving Mexican-American fifth graders, working as tutors, shared books with first grade students they tutored and then asked the first graders to react to the books by writing or drawing. As the fifth graders worked with their young students, researchers and teachers began to notice changes in the older youngsters' behavior. Their attitudes toward reading became more positive. They requested library cards and began taking books to the cafeteria to read at lunch time. The intermediate grade children, who had not thought of themselves as readers, began to see themselves in a different light.

From this initial project where students had the opportunity to enjoy books and read for authentic purposes, Fair Oaks moved into a literature-based reading program. Teachers began to question the instructional assumption of reading as a series of subskills that needed to be mastered in a highly controlled format before real stories could be read (Franklin, 1986). Instead, in a literature-based approach to literacy, children read literature of various types rather than basal reader stories. Some of the literature was student-selected and some teacher-selected.

Such an approach, advocated here as an optimal way of connecting reading and writing for second language learners, is based on the fundamental premise that for both oral and written language acquisition, in either a first or a second language, language is best learned when it is being used for something else. That is, language is acquired for what it can do for the learner (Edelsky, in press-b). This means that just as a person learns to talk by talking for various purposes, a person learns to read by reading and by being read to

(Smith, 1982). Children become readers, according to this perspective, not because they are drilled in the variety of subskills presented in a basal reader series, but because they read books that are interesting, meaningful, and aesthetically pleasing. And children become lovers of books rather than reluctant readers (Flores et al., 1985).

Another premise that highlights a literature-based approach to reading is that reading is viewed as a means of studying literature, rather than literature viewed as a means of studying reading (Edelsky, in press-c). Thus, for example, children read *Charlotte's Web* and reflect upon it in discussions, sharing their feelings about the book in its entirety and, for example, considering how E.B. White developed characters, or how he used descriptions to paint a picture of Wilbur, or how he used foreshadowing to hint at what would happen to Charlotte. This contrasts dramatically with reading the same book (or a selection from it) and answering recall questions about what happened, or putting sentences that summarize events from the book into their proper sequence, or defining "new" vocabulary from the context of sentences pulled from the story. In this view, literature is used as a way of knowing and learning, both aesthetically and analytically (Bird & Alvarez, 1987; Edelsky, in press-b).

Literary analysis is carried out through what are called literature study groups. In literature study, a small group of children read the same book and meet one or two times a week with the teacher to share their impressions and personal reactions to the story and to analyze the author's writing craft. The group considers such aspects of the book as character, setting, plot, and theme. The group may also consider how the writer uses narration, description, and so on, focusing on the language of the author as well as on the ways in which the author makes the book come together to form a satisfying experience for the reader (Edelsky, in press-c; Flores et al., 1985; Samway & Alvarez, 1987).

In another specific consideration of the reading-writing connection, one kind of writing that is often used in literature-based classrooms is what is called a literature log or journal (Flores et al., 1985; Freeman & Freeman, in press). A literature log is similar to a journal or diary (and generally promotes the same kind of expressive writing), but instead of being general in content it is focused specifically on the story that the child is reading. The purpose of a literature log is to give readers a means to reflect on what they are reading by spending a few minutes discussing, in writing, the meaning of the book. Here, they include the relationship between the story and their own personal experiences. Within literature-based classrooms, the teacher often reads and responds to student literature logs in much the same way as to dialogue journals. Particularly when the teacher has read the book, the log may take on the flavor of a written conversation, as two readers share the meanings that they have created from a book. The example below is a demonstration of such sharing. (Flores et al., 1985):

Child's entry:

The way I felt about Where the Red Fern
Grows it was very sad my tears wanted to
come out but the colden't especially
when old Dan and little Ann died. They
were such pretty brown dogs. I wish I
could have both of them Both of them
were such good little dogs. I thought
the Red Fern was very pretty. When I
began to cry I could feel like if there
was a big rock stuk in my throat.

Teacher's entry:

I cried, too, Jennifer. When Little Ann
was lying on top of the grave of Old Dan
my mouth got very dry as if I hadn't had
a drink of water in over a week. I
couldn't stop crying.

From *Holistic Bilingual Instructional Strategies* by B. Flores et al. Phoenix, AZ: Exito, 1985. Copyright by Exito and the authors. Reprinted with permission of the authors.

While the major goal of a literature-based program is that children come to appreciate literature in and of itself, there is also evidence that the literary analyses that learners carry out have a carryover effect on their writing, resulting in better quality poetic/literary writing and in conferencing about writing that includes many of the same aspects that have been considered in examining a professional author's work (Edelsky, in press-c; Samway & Alvarez, 1987). When they create literary efforts, children bring to that task what they have learned about the author's craft. So as they create drafts, and as they reflect on their own and others' work, they consider their own work from an author's point of view. They thus begin to "write like readers" (Smith, 1982). This is what Heath (1985) refers to as "literate behavior," using language to talk about language, using language to critique the language of student creations.

Transactional Writing

The last category of writing delineated by Britton is what he calls transactional writing, expository or informational writing with a focus on presenting something clearly to a reader. This is writing to get things done (Smith, 1982). Berthoff (1981) wisely points out that there are many varying definitions of expository writing, which means that one problem associated with expository writing is how to define it. While definitions vary, probably many educators would agree that some of the functions that this kind of writing would serve are, for example, to present information, to make a series of points, to summarize, to raise questions, to answer questions, to present a particular point of view, to persuade the reader to adopt an idea or a stance, to give an opinion and back it up, and so on. In school, this kind of writing is often associated with content areas such as social studies, science, mathematics, and health, where students may be asked to summarize and/or interpret content material, collect and organize information about a topic, explain steps in an experiment or problem, delineate steps taken and results, state conclusions and speculate as to why certain results came out as they did, and take a position and defend it.

There is evidence that, in school settings, elementary-school-age children move gradually into this kind of writing. Their writing typically combines expository writing, the presentation of facts, with more personal expressive writing, the expression of feelings about or reactions to what is being written. Thus, children's writing often combines elements of expressive and expository writing (Britton, et al., 1975). Oljean (1984) and Jacobs (1984) have found that when children are asked to write informational pieces, they often combine personal expression and narrative along with information, jointly making use of narration and opinion as one way of conveying information. Similar phenomena have been noted for ESL learners (Hudelson, 1986). Jacobs suggests that, in terms of children's cognitive development, it may be both inappropriate and counterproductive to push children to write expository or informational prose as adults do. Rather, as children venture into expository, informational writing they should be able to combine their presentation of facts with personal reflections. This will lead, eventually, to a cleaner separation of exposition and personal expression.

Because of a fundamental agreement with Jacob's position, this monograph does not take the position that expository writing, as it is viewed by those working with secondary students and adults, should be taught to elementary school ESL learners. But it seems to make sense to involve children in writing opportunities that move them toward informational, expository writing. They can begin to understand the difference between expository writing and fictional or reflective writing. The rest of this chapter will consider ways to move toward expository and informational writing that are appropriate for elementary school children.

One way to move toward expository and informational writing is to use the content areas of the elementary school curriculum, including meaningful writing activities, as an integral part of content area work. The position that content areas may be used for second language development is one that has received considerable attention recently (Chamot & O'Malley, 1987; Crandall, 1987; Hudelson, 1988b; Mohan, 1986). Because ESL children eventually must deal with content material in English, and because recent second language research suggests that language is learned most effectively when it is being used to accomplish something other than to focus on the language per se, content area study has come to be seen as an appropriate vehicle for ESL development. Given this reality, it is appropriate to ask how content areas can be used for writing development, and how content area activities can be organized to include writing.

The first way in which writing may be incorporated into content areas is to include it as a part of ongoing class activities in various content areas. In one bilingual fourth grade classroom, for example, the second language learners had raised white rats named Roy and Rosemary. The children became involved in learning about the rats, and the teacher suggested that some of the students might want to spend some time each day observing Roy and Rosemary, finding out about them by conducting "experiments" and writing down their observations, so that they would have a record of what they were doing and learning. Some of the children chose to do this. A look at part of one child's log of observations reveals the child using writing to record what he observed, to describe what the children were trying to find out about the rats, and to explain both what they discovered and why they did not succeed. This is the beginning of writing to present information.

Early Expository Writing

February 27
Roy and Rosemary are in the cage that has food in it. Roy was in the cage eating his food and Rosemary was feeding. Then Elsa got Roy and got a ruler and got Roy and Roy scratched her then Elsa didn't want to get them because they scratch her. Then we went and got some gloves from Candy and we weighed the rats but the ras kept on moving so we didn't weigh them right.

March 4
Today we measured them they both weigh 35 decimeter and we also weighed them. Roy weigh 6 oz. 5 washers Rosemary weighed 5 oz 6 washers so Roy weighed more than Rosemary

March 5
Today we made a maze and put them in their. Roy and Rosemary

couldn't find the way out because it was hard to get out of their because we put a lot of book everywhere. We put Roy inside the maze and he couldn't find his way out and we put Rosemary and the same thing happened to her

In another setting, a teacher in a self-contained ESL class was working on career awareness as a part of the social studies curriculum. This teacher decided to create a class bulletin board based on children's career choices. So the children were asked to write about their career goals and to illustrate their choices. The first drafts that the children produced demonstrate that, even with limited control over English, they were able to use the language to explain why they were interested in specific careers. They could begin to use writing to explain some of their ideas to other people.

Writing to Make a Point

I lake to vi secretarian becaese dad the
I lake to be becase is pretty to be
secretarian

When I be big I want to be a scientis
becaus they mate thinge real good

When I gow up I whant to be a teacher
to teach chirdrens

I would like to be a doctor to help
people that are sick. Being a doctor is
nice and helpful. I will operate people
that need operation and that are haveing
a baby for me is a good career.

I want to be a maganic. I love to work
in maganic. When I grow up I going to
work maganic. I don't forget the
maganic.

The department of government that keeps
order investigates creims and makes
arres the members of this department is
in a city. I would like to be a police
officer.

Another way to approach content area writing is to begin with content area objectives, which are probably familiar to teachers in school districts in many places. Using instructional objectives rather than text material, it is possible to organize activities for learners that would focus on both the content area objective and provide for some writing connected to the content activities (Hudelson, 1988b). The first example comes from elementary school science and is concerned with the study of light and shadow. The objective reads: Children will observe the changes in shadows during the course of the day.

Initially, addressing the objective involves planning an activity or activities that will enable children to investigate shadows and to carry out some writing as an integral part of the activity, such as children measuring their shadows. To accomplish this, children's attention can be focused on two questions: Is your shadow the same size that you are? What happens to the length of your shadow if it is measured at different times of the day? Children can predict (orally, or preferably in writing) the answers to these questions. Then children can be divided into groups. Each group can be responsible for going outside (or to an appropriate place where their shadows may be seen) and measuring each group member's shadow. This information can be written down on a chart created for the activity (writing, in this case, serving as a memory aid and record of what was done in each group). The chart could have two columns labeled: How tall am I? What's the length of my shadow? When all of the groups have completed their measuring, each can share its results and the class can compare the predictions that had been made about Question 1 with the results of their experiment.

Following this discussion the learners can respond in writing to questions such as: What did you learn today? What questions do you have? These responses are done in what some have called content journals or learning logs (Freeman & Freeman, in press; Fulwiler,

1987). Learning logs are like personal journals in that each learner writes from an individual perspective, but they are different from personal journals in that they focus on content being studied. They ask learners to consider what they are studying in a content area and to try to make sense of it. Learning logs also give learners the opportunity to ask questions about what they don't understand. Usually learning logs or content journals are shared with the teacher, so that the teacher has a clearer sense of what the learners understand in the content area.

On another day (or several days), the learners, again in groups, can compare the lengths of their shadows at one time of day to the lengths at another time (for example, when school starts and when school ends), again using predicting, charting, comparing, and reflecting in writing in their content journals.

From these activities comes an experiential understanding of the changes in shadow over time. Children can then read about shadows, using sources such as the text (but not being limited to this one source), children's informational books from the library, children's science magazines, and so on. These sources might also enable learners (working individually or in groups) to create books such as *My First Book About Shadows*. Using writing workshop processes, students can draft and revise their own informational books, with the materials that they are reading as models. This gives students another opportunity to move into expository, informational writing.

In social studies, too, instructional objectives may be used as a springboard for writing. For example, intermediate grade objectives that focus on the concept of immigration could be used. Students will be able to explain that the people of the United States are immigrants linked to the rest of the world through their ancestral heritages, and students will be able to tell how their own ancestral heritages link them to the rest of the world.

A variety of activities that include writing might enable ESL learners to meet these objectives. A logical place to begin the study of immigration might be with something in or close to the children's own experiences: their family's immigration to this country. Initially learners can work in groups to arrive at a set of questions that they ask their families about how, when, and why they came to this country. At home, students can either use their own information to arrive at answers to the questions, or they can interview a family member and jot down answers to the questions. After collecting information about their families, learners divide into groups to share what they have learned and to create group charts that summarize each group's information. Maps are then used to locate the countries of the children's ancestors. The routes that the immigrants took to the United States can be drawn.

Several other related projects can be undertaken. Children might construct their own family or individual autobiographies, first representing important events on a timeline and then creating chapters depicting the timeline events. Groups of learners can investigate a variety of immigrant groups to this country to learn more about heritage and contributions to this country. Information is collected from multiple sources, and reports can be written to share with others. The report writing should involve the creation of initial drafts, sharing what has been written, and revising and editing (Hudelson, 1988b). These activities demonstrate that written language development may be an integral part of school content and content area objectives.

Using Thematic Units

In addition to thinking about content area work from the point of view of objectives, it is possible to approach it from the perspective of thematic units. Thematic unit teaching involves organizing sets of instructional activities around content topics or themes of interest and relevance to children, for example, dinosaurs, space, holidays, cowboys, and communities. The activities that the teacher organizes require that children, working in groups as well as independently, use oral and written language for varied purposes as they explore the topic. The approach is not based on answering questions in textbooks, but rather on exploring problems and seeking answers to questions through activities that require children to work collaboratively. In their explorations of content, children use all of the language processes. The language processes are viewed both as inseparable from one another and as the means through which children explore content. Language grows because children use it as a means to an end, the end being learning about an interesting topic. Children are engaged in finding out about the world, and language is one of the vehicles through which to explore (Allen & Hudelson, 1986).

An example of a unit may make the ideas clearer. The topic of the unit is the zoo. In this unit, using pictures, books, filmstrips, their own background knowledge, and their experiences at the zoo, the children examine and compare familiar and unfamiliar animals. They categorize animals according to their skin and appendages and investigate the ways in which such animals protect themselves. They read about animals in children's literature and create some of their own animal tales. They use mapping to plan their route to the zoo and to plot their way through the zoo. They spend a day at the zoo, which includes a talk and hands-on experience with some animals conducted by a zoo docent. They create a mural about the trip. In carrying out these activities, children use language for planning, for describing, for narrating, for predicting, for comparing, and for giving and accepting directions.

How specifically does writing fit into this unit? In many ways. Some of the children create a chart on which they record the names of the animals they see and the kinds of feet each animal has. Later, several of the beginning ESL children draw pictures of many of the animals and write brief descriptions of what they have seen to accompany their drawings. These are placed around the classroom.

The teachers also illustrate part of the craft of writing by using some of the children's longer descriptions to work on revision. In examining these pieces, the teachers discover that the texts list information about the animals but provide little organization. Most of the writing focuses on what the animal looks like and what the animal does. The teachers ask the children who have copies of the drafts and marker pens, to underline in red all the sentences that describe the animal's appearance and to underline in blue all the sentences that describe the animal's behavior. Then the children cut the sentences apart and rearrange them to form new paragraphs. Sometimes words are added or deleted. Sometimes new information is included. This task of revising creates a real purpose to use language and to talk about language. There is a reason to discuss both meaning and form (Allen & Hudelson, 1986).

Finally, several class books are made, so that the writing takes a final "published" form. The children work in groups to organize each book by sequencing the pages, mounting the illustrations, and arranging the text.

Writing may also be used as a tool for facilitating construction of meaning from content area textbooks. Since a reader's comprehension of text depends partially on the reader's prior knowledge of the subject (Barnitz, 1985), it is important to activate that prior knowledge before reading. One way to do this is to ask readers, perhaps in a learning log or content journal format, to write down what they already know about what they are going to read. Following this pre-reading activity, learners read and discuss the assigned text. After the reading, learners again write about the topic, this time using what they have learned from the reading as well as their prior knowledge. This activity, called a *Guided Writing Procedure*, has been found to be an effective way to assist second language learners in content area work (Searfoss, Smith & Bean, 1981). The example below illustrates how much the reader learned about Columbus from reading and discussing the text (Searfoss, Smith & Bean, 1981, p. 390).

Day 1 - before reading text

> His name is columbs. He was born in Italy and thin he went to queen to aske four some mony and thin the qeen by tree sheep four him the neme of the sheep is Nina) Pinta P Santa Maria and think he find a gold and he went to new world.

Day 3 - after reading and discussing text

> He is name christopher colmbs. Ge was born in Italy. He as a weaver. His broth was a map maker. He dreameaed of a fantastic voyage to the Far East. He became a master seaman. He stayed in Lisbon because he was shipwrecked. He ask the quen of the Spian four three sheep. the name of the three are Nina) Pinta) and (Santa Maria)
> He went fo find a gold in India and China He discovered San Salvador, Cuba, Hispaniola and puerto Rico. columbus kid-

napped (natives) from the New Land. He died in 1500 and judyed a falur.

> From "An Integrated Language Strategy for the Second Language Learners" by L. Searfoss, C. Smith & T. Bean. *TESOL Quarterly, 15*, 383-392. Copyright 1981 by Searfoss, Smith, & Bean. Reprinted with permission.

Published descriptions of this activity suggest that learners turn in their writing to the teacher for editing of form. In thinking about the activity from the perspectives both of content learning and of purposeful and authentic language, it would make more sense to ask learners to share their writing with each other, both prior to and after reading about the topic. Before reading, groups of students, through sharing their writing, can pool their ideas and create several lists of what students say that they already knew about Columbus. After reading and writing, students can again pool their knowledge to see if there is more information to add to the list. They can also examine their original lists to make sure that their prior knowledge was accurate, that is, that it was not contradicted by something in the reading. In these ways writing can be used as a basis for discussion and consideration of content, rather than as a way to correct errors.

Finally, expository, informational writing may be encouraged through children creating texts (for example, books or reports) on topics of their own choice and using many of the previously described writing workshop processes as they work. Nations (1986) has described a project that involved second grade native speakers and ESL learners in preparing informational books on their favorite animals. In order to produce their books, the children have to accomplish the following: They choose animals they want to write about; they brainstorm questions they will research; they seek information from varied sources; they take notes from their resources; they work on drafts of their books; they share their drafts and make revisions based on others' suggestions; they produce final versions of books that become a part of the class library and then of the school library; and they read their books to other classes. Nations found that frequently the children work together, and that the more fluent English speakers and readers often help their friends to collect information and to produce their drafts.

Kitagawa (in press) describes a similar project carried out with sixth graders. Once the children choose and research their own topics, Kitagawa uses the drafting, sharing, and revising processes that the children normally use as a part of writer's workshop. Students craft their reports for an authentic audience of their peers. They become researchers of a topic of genuine interest to them; they set questions and find answers; they create works designed to present information clearly to other readers.

Summary

The purpose of this chapter has been to offer a variety of strategies that teachers might use to incorporate writing into classroom activities for their second language learners. These strategies are summarized:

1) Use diaries or journals both to promote fluency in writing and to help students see writing as one means of self-expression.

2) Utilize personal narratives and writing workshop techniques in order to help learners become comfortable with writing on self-selected topics and with drafting, sharing, and revising their pieces, while viewing writing as a craft.

3) Make the reading-writing connection by exposing ESL learners to a wide variety of literary forms in reading and then asking students to use their growing knowledge of various genres to construct their own literary forms to share with others.

4) Incorporate expressive, literary, and expository writing into meaningful content area learning, so that ESL learners begin to experience the kind of writing that will be expected of them in disciplines across the curriculum.

This chapter began with a perspective on writing instruction for ESL learners based on the *whole language* perspective that written language is acquired through meaningful use. A particularly clear explication of *whole language* principles applied to second language literacy has been prepared by Freeman & Freeman (in press). This chapter closes with these principles because they provide an excellent way of thinking about classroom instruction and the writing development of ESL learners.

The principles are the following:

1) Classrooms should be learner-centered.

2) Learning progresses from whole to part.

3) Learning is enhanced through the use of all four modes: reading, writing, speaking, and listening.

4) People learn things that serve their own purposes.

5) Learning occurs during social interactions.

6) Teachers must have faith that their students can and will learn.

4
Assessing Children's Writing

The assessment of student learning is an important part of the activity of elementary schools, one that is central to the enterprise of schooling. Critics frequently suggest that schools are so obsessed with assessment that little else happens in many schools. Even critics would agree, however, that there is a genuine need to examine how children progress, how they grow intellectually, how and what they learn. Schools and teachers have an obligation to themselves, to colleagues and superiors, to parents, and to the learners themselves, to document what children have learned and achieved. This obligation is as true for writing as it is for other areas of the curriculum.

The purpose of this chapter is to address educators' concerns and needs to assess and document ESL children's progress in writing. The emphasis in this chapter is on assessment based on daily classroom activity, as much as possible, rather than on contrived situations or standardized achievement tests. The perspective taken is that assessment should be based on observation and documentation of what children do in authentic writing contexts in their classrooms (Genishi and Dyson, 1984; Graves, 1983).

In addition, the following questions must be considered: 1) For whom is the assessment done? 2) Why make the assessment? Three major groups concerned with assessment are teachers, the children themselves, and others concerned with student progress, such as parents and school administrators. The rest of this chapter will be organized around possible assessment strategies useful and/or relevant to these groups of individuals.

Writing Assessment and the Classroom Teacher

Clearly, one of the persons most concerned with children's progress in the classroom is the teacher. Teachers want and need to know how their students are doing, what they are learning and what they are having trouble with, how they are reacting to classroom instruction, what they are enjoying, and finally, how they have been learning and changing over time. Teachers need this kind of information in order to plan future instruction. They also need the information in order to communicate accurately and effectively with parents about the progress of their children, and in order to work constructively with colleagues and supervisors who are also concerned with children's progress. Teachers, then, are especially concerned about ways to document both student progress and needs.

The logical place to gather information about writing is from the learners' daily writing. Classroom teachers need to keep multiple samples of their students' writing. If the children keep journals, diaries, literature or learning logs, these need to be collected and saved. If children participate in writers' workshop activities or if they work on expository or informational pieces, both assigned and unassigned, they need folders in which to store their finished and unfinished pieces. To make fair assessments, teachers need multiple examples of a child's writing.

In addition to collecting writing samples, teachers must decide how to look at what they have gathered. Many educators decide to use checklists or forms to examine children's writing and to record specific aspects of writing development (Genishi & Dyson, 1984). Teachers develop checklists that focus on aspects of writing that they judge to be important for their learners and/or that they are emphasizing in writing instruction. Teachers focus on aspects that depend on the age, English language development, and writing experiences of the child. For example, Flores et al. (1985) provide examples of two checklists appropriate for use with interactive journals, one for use with kindergarten and first-grade beginning writers and one for use with fourth through sixth grade students. They advocate using journal entries to assess both what they term quality of writing and mechanical aspects of composition.

Name _____ Age _____ Grade _____

First Grade & K Evaluation Summary of Interactive Journal Writing
Developed by: Dr. Barbara Flores and Erminda Garcia

Quality of Writing	Date														
Language of Writing (E, S, or S/E)	C	D	NE	C	D	NE	C	D	NE	C	D	NE	C	D	NE
Understand purpose															
Willing to take risks															
Uses Journal as a reference															
Type of writing system used															
Self corrects writing															
Can read back own writing															
Shares journal with peers															
Expresses thoughts															
Mechanics															
% of invented spelling															
# of invented															
# of total words															
% of conventionally spelled															
Uses left-to-right directionality															
Uses paper conventionally															
Uses conv. letter formation															
Handles pencil convention.															
Uses punctuation															
Uses lower case															
Uses upper case															
Spaces conventionally															

Comments _____

_____

_____

_____

_____

Legend:
P/S - Use of presyllabic writing system   S/A - Use of syllabic/alphabetic writing system
S - Use of syllabic writing system   A - Use of alphabetic writing system
          C - Controls   D - Developing   NE - No Evidence   NA - Not Applicable

Figure 1. Checklist for Interactive Journal Writing
From *Holistic Bilingual Instructional Strategies* (p.10) by B. Flores et al., 1985, Phoenix, AZ: Exito. Copyright 1985 by Exito. Used with permission.

Teacher _____

Name _____ Age _____ Grade _____

Pine Hill Schools
An Evaluation to Document Children's Literacy Development
Interactive Journal Writing   Grades 4th, 5th, 6th

Quality of Writing   Date

	C	D	NE	C	D	NE	C	D	NE	C	D	NE	C	D	NE
Self Selects Topics															
Uses Expansive Vocabulary															
Uses Complex Sentences															
Experiments with Different Styles															
Revision Strategies															

Mechanics

Handwriting
Spelling
  Invented _____ %
  Conventional _____ %
  Total _____ %
Punctuation
Capitalization
Grammar Usage

(EXAMPLE watermark across grid)

Comments _____
_____
_____
_____
_____

D - Developing   C - Controls   NE - No Evidence

Figure 2. Checklist for Interactive Journal Writing (Intermediate)
From *Holistic Bilingual Instructional Strategies* (p.11) by B. Flores et al., 1985, Phoenix, AZ: Exito. Copyright by Exito. Used with permission.

Child's Name	Appears to write letters randomly	Writes letters for syllables	Writes visually-recalled pattern	Requests spellings	Spelling Phonologically -based on letter names	-based on consonant sounds
Rachel	10/8		10/14 Julie (her sister)	10/20 - peers' names		
Vivi	10/14	10/17	10/8 - family names		10/23 - combines this & syl. method	
Nate			10/14 - peers' names			10/8 - does w/ ease

Date entered when behavior first noted.

The behaviors listed are possible encoding strategies. No fixed developmental sequence is implied.

Figure 3. Checklist for Recording Children's Encoding Strategies
From *Language Assessment in the Early Years* (p. 183) by C. Genishi & A. Dyson, 1984, Norwood,NJ: Ablex Publishing. Copyright 1984 by Ablex. Used with permission.

Names	Begins sentence with a capital letter	Ends sentence with a period	Ends question with a question mark	Uses commas in a list	Uses apostrophes in contractions
Diane	✓+	✓+	✓+	✓+	✓
Efren	✓	✓	✓	✓	✓
Robert	✓+	✓+	✓	-	-
Ruth Ann	✓	✓	✓+	-	-
Becky	✓+	✓+	-	-	✓

Key: ✓+ always
✓ sometimes
- random or never

Figure 4. Checklist for Evaluating Use of Written Conventions
From *Language Assessment in the Early Years* (p.239) by C. Genishi & A. Dyson, 1984, Norwood, NJ: Ablex Publishing. Copyright 1984 by Ablex. Used with permission.

Observations about the Student as a Learner
Supplementary Reading Program Report

Reading Specialist: Janis Bailey

Student: _____ Year _____ Grade _____

			1	2	3	4
Seems to view self as an effective reader		during shared reading				
		during independent reading				
Seems to view self as an effective author		when dictating writing				
		during independent writing				
Takes Risks: As a reader in:	–selecting books					
	–predicting	using knowledge in own head (prior experience)				
		using text and/or pictures				
	–figuring out unknowns: using meaning clues	in context				
		in own head (prior experience)				
	using sentence structure clues (grammer, etc.)					
	substituting a word with similar meaning					
	using "sounding out"					
	using word structure clues (endings, basewords, etc.)					
	–revising thinking when "it doesn't make sense"					
	–talking meaningfully about books	in retelling material read				
		in group discussions, sharing				
As a writer in:	–choosing writing topics					
	–producing meaningful writing					
	–spelling with invented spelling to maintain meaning					
	–revising writing to make it more meaningful					
	–sharing own writing					
Chooses to pursue topics of interest						
Uses a variety of resources and literature to learn about self-selected topics						
Sticks with a plan	in reading					
	in writing					
Raises questions:	about books read or listened to by the student					
	about information others share in group					
	that may lead to new learning					

☑ Effectively demonstrated by the student at this time   ■ Not a focus at this time.

Figure 5. Checklist that Includes the Idea of Risktaking in Writing
From Problem solving our way to alternative evaluation procedures by J. Bailey et al., 1988, *Language Arts*, 65 (4), p.367. Copyright 1988 by National Council of Teachers of English. Used with permission.

Figure 6. Checklist of Literacy Development: Reading and Writing Strategies (overleaf)
From Problem solving our way to alternative evaluation procedures by J. Bailey et al., 1988, *Language Arts*, 65 (4), p.367. Copyright 1988 by National Council of Teachers of English. Used with permission.

TRANSITIONAL LITERACY DEVELOPMENT CHECKLIST
Observations and Student Behavior

Student _____ Teacher _____

Observations About...	Date	Contextual Notes
I. Interest in Books		
demonstrates interest in books		
samples different genre		
uses library		
engages in spontaneous book talk		
brings additional books to class		
II. Book Knowledge and Library Skills		
external organization—narrative		
external organization—expository		
demonstrates use of...		
–glossary		
–encyclopedia		
–dictionary		
–card catalog		
–alphabetical ordering		
can choose appropriate books		
III. Reading Comprehension		
adequate retelling of story or major events		
demonstrates understanding of...		
–plot		
–main idea		
–characters		
–setting		
–climax		
can interpret figurative language		
differentiates fact and opinoin		
fact and fiction		
when questioned, can make comparison		
–show cause and effect		
–predict outcomes		
–begin to make inferences		
can identify mood and tone		
reads familiar material fluently suitable intonations and phrasing		
can use text to support statements		
makes connections to own experiences		
views reding as a predictive process		
knowledge of story structure		
uses prior knowledge		
IV. Reading Strategies		
self-corrects when meaning is lost		
When encountering unfamiliar words...		
–returns to beginning of sent/phrase		
–uses pictures and other support clues		
–makes use of reference tools		

Observations About... (continued)	Date	Contextual Notes
makes integrated use of semantic and syntactic cueing systems		
makes use of graphophonic cueing		
increases sight word vocabulary		
adjusts speed of reading to material		
declining use of voice or finger as fluency increases		
observes punctuation to obtain meaning		
knows how to skim material		
previews text for general content		
reads silently with greater ease		
reads familiar material fluently		
uses organization of text to read content material		
substitutes word(s) making syntactic or semantic sense for unknown word(s)		
will skip a word and read on		
views self as an effective reader		
takes risks in... –predicting		
–pronunciation		
–discussion		
uses prior knowledge		
V. Writing Strategies		
takes risk in spelling		
sharing own writing		
length of text		
generates topics and writing ideas		
willingly shares writing		
willingness to edit (–makes contextual changes)		
develops revising skills (editing)		
–proofreading skills		
makes conventional use of... –capitals		
–question marks		
–possessives		
–contractions		
–apostrophes		
–paragraphing		
attempts spelling generalizations		
begins to use dialogue		
makes use of descriptive language		
is developing awareness of audience		
demonstrates development of topic		
uses forms appropriate to purpose		
views self as effective writer		
uses prior knowledge		

For these checklists, teachers have determined what specific aspects of writing will be evaluated. An examination of the checklists (Figures 1 and 2) reveals differing expectations for primary and intermediate level students, expectations based on teachers' continuing work with learners.

Flores et al. (1985) advocate that teachers, when using these checklists to assess or document writing development, make periodic examinations of children's journals, and document whether learners control (c) or are developing (d) specific aspects of writing, or whether the category is not applicable (na) or whether no evidence is available (ne). Such systematic observation and documentation done several times during the year, will enable teachers to chart and demonstrate children's progress. Teachers will also be able to identify specific aspects of writing that they may need to teach.

The checklist categories listed above are certainly not a definitive list of aspects of writing that teachers might wish to assess. Genishi & Dyson (1984) also offer alternatives for checklists, suggesting that teachers of young children may want to develop several forms, each of which concentrates on a different aspect of writing. For example, the authors offer a checklist (Figure 3) for use in assessing children's developing strategies for encoding print. They suggest that teachers use the categories to note the date when they first observe the child exhibiting the writing behavior in a piece of writing.

Genishi & Dyson (1984) also have developed a sample checklist (Figure 4) for assessment of children's control over conventions of written language, including capitalization and punctuation.

In a recent collaborative effort, several teachers worked together to develop checklists for documenting children's progress as writers (Bailey et al., 1988). One checklist focused on the child's view of himself as writer, and on this writer as risk-taker. This checklist has been reproduced as Figure 5. Another checklist considered various writing strategies that child writers might exhibit as they develop writing ability. This checklist has been reproduced as Figure 6.

These checklists demonstrate that it is possible to assess more global as well as more specific aspects of children's writing. From these samples, it should be obvious that checklists will vary widely. What the checklists have in common is that they represent one way for teachers to assess their children's writing efforts in organized ways and to document both child development and some of their instructional needs. Teacher-created and -adapted checklists also are important because teachers may assess what they believe are important aspects of writing for their own classes of children.

Checklists are not the only tool available to teachers who wish to assess their students' growing abilities as writers. Graves (1983) believes that teachers should keep notes and anecdotal records on their students. One place where observing and notetaking may form an integral part of writing instruction is during and after individual and group writing conferences with children. These notes, which some teachers keep as part of each child's writing folder, may highlight a specific writing skill that teacher and child(ren) worked on in a conference or small group session. The notes may also reflect the teacher's awareness of something not previously found in the child's writing efforts. An example of this is the child who begins to take risks with writing where previously he or she had not felt comfortable enough to do so. When added to the data from checklists and other observations, such anecdotal records provide a more accurate picture of writing development than do checklists or forms alone.

Graves (1983) is not satisfied with assessing children through notes and checklists that focus on children's written products. He advocates (as do Genishi & Dyson, 1984) that teachers develop their observational skills so they will be better able to know where children are in their writing, not only in terms of writing products and mini-lessons but also in terms of process and classroom context. In thinking about observation, Graves lays out possibilities for varied observations.

> **Folder observation** - The teacher looks over a child's writing folder or writing samples the night before observing that child during writing time in class.
>
> **Distant observation** - The teacher stands at the side of the room and observes a specific child's behavior during a few minutes of writing. The teacher can look at the child's posture and positioning, the child's use of various resources, the child's relationship

to other children, the child's movement, and the child's actual writing time.

Close-in observation - The teacher sits next to a child as he writes. The teacher examines the child's use of the space on the page, the child's handling of writing problems, and the child's switch from speech to print.

Participant observation - This method moves beyond close-in observation. The teacher questions the child about his writing, in order to try to answer questions that cannot be answered simply by observing. The teacher may ask the child, for example, how he was able to spell a specific work correctly, how he decided what he would write next, how he tackled certain problems in his writing.

Readers of this chapter who are classroom teachers may be asking where they are going to get the time to carry out such extensive observations. Graves readily acknowledges that these observations will not take place frequently for each child in the class. He does advocate that teachers spend as little as five minutes daily in observations and in recording observations. Even though these detailed observations will be infrequent, they will provide insights into strategies and processes the child is using. These strategies and processes may not be obvious if teachers examine only the child's products. These observations offer a richer assessment of a child's development as a writer.

Writing Assessment and the Child

Donald Graves begins his discussion of classroom writing assessment with the statement "Teachers and children need to have a sense of where they are" (Graves, 1983, p. 295). Graves takes the position that both teacher and child need a sense of the child's progress and what the child is accomplishing in writing. In order for children to develop confidence as writers, they need evidence of what they have learned and what they need to work on. Assessment, in the sense of documentation of strengths and needs, is thus important for children as well as for adults.

One way in which children can develop a sense of where they are in writing is through access to their work (both completed and in progress) and through access the teacher's records, whether these records be in the form of checklists or notes. Teachers can provide access to student and teacher materials and notes by creating folders for each child. These folders can contain forms, checklists, conference notes, and the students' writing. The children can look at their own writing and at the teacher's notes. From this, they will have a clear sense of where they have been, how they have progressed, and where they may want to go.

Children should be a part of the assessment process. This gives them a way to see their writing style. While it may be surprising to some, researchers working both with native English speakers and with ESL learners have demonstrated that children are able to evaluate their own work and are able to explain their ratings (Hilgers, 1986; Samway, 1987b). Samway (1987b) asked ESL learners to separate stories into three piles: those they considered very good, okay, and not so good. She then asked the children to explain why they had judged certain stories as they had. Samway found that the children judged the stories through retelling (making comments that paraphrased the story); liking (making comments that reflected personal liking of an element in the text); surface features (focusing on such forms of the text as spelling, handwriting, and length); understanding (efforts on the reader's part to make sense of the text); crafting (commenting on things that the author had done to draft the piece such as describe or explain); value-related (comments about what a piece intended to do, such as teach you something); entertainment (the degree to which a text generated an emotional response); nonfictional/fictional (concern with whether a story is based on reality or not); and audience reaction (whether an audience liked the story).

Given that children are able to make judgments about their work, it seems sensible to ask learners to add their assessments to those of their teachers. At the elementary school level, this might be accomplished by using a modified version of a portfolio assessment. Every several months, children could be asked to choose three or four examples of their best work, and then to explain how they made a choice. The teacher could take notes on the learner's comments, and these would form part of the assessment records kept for each child. In addition, or as an alternative, learners could be asked, periodically, to review their work, to reflect on how their writing had changed, and to examine their pieces in order to comment on what they had learned to do as writers. This reflection could be done with the teacher or with another student. Some children might be able to write down some of what they had learned on a form titled perhaps, *What I Know About Writing* or *Writing Skills I Can Use*. Other children could respond to a writing skills checklist. They could check off the skills that are demonstrated in their work. In like fashion, children might be asked periodically to list or talk about what they still need to work on or what they want to learn next.

Whatever procedures are created, it makes sense to include children's judgments of their strengths and weaknesses in any assessment of their writing. It also seems to make sense to ask children to assume some of the responsibility for identifying what they know and what they feel they still need to learn. If teachers do believe that their students can and will learn (Freeman & Freeman, in press), asking them to take some responsibility for their learning is one way of demonstrating this trust.

From the Outside Looking in

In addition to teachers and students, there are others who are concerned about the development of the child as a writer. Parents, curriculum supervisors, and district and state superintendents are among those who keep a concerned eye on student writing. Teachers must share their ongoing assessment records with these audiences.

Parents of second language learners are largely concerned about their child's improvement; they ask about progress. If parents see the collection of writing samples of their children, they can witness the development of writing skills (recall the examples from fifth grader Betty's journal in chapter one of this volume). Teachers should consider showing parents the forms and checklists that indicate skills development and progress.

Parents will undoubtedly have questions about the writing "errors" that they see. Teachers must articulate language learning theories (including the general principle that both oral and written language learning involves making mistakes) and use learner's writing samples to make their points clear. This explanation is essential even if it must be accomplished through a translator.

Supervisors and administrators may share many of the same concerns as parents. They want evidence that children are learning, and in the case of writing, that they are learning to write effectively. Since definitions of effective writing may vary, teachers engaged in the kinds of process writing advocated in this monograph need to be able to articulate their definitions of writing and writing progress to their colleagues. They need to be able to explain their writing program and, through the records that they have collected, their children's progress. Teachers of second language learners may also need to share with their colleagues the kind of perspective on second language literacy acquisition presented in this and other volumes (Edelsky, 1986; Enright & McCloskey, 1988; Flores et al., 1985; Rigg & Enright, 1986).

In many school districts, curriculum supervisors have developed lists of specific objectives for the content areas. These objectives reflect the district's attempt to outline the most basic learning in each curricular area at each grade level. In language arts these objectives inevitably include writing objectives, objectives that often give consideration to more global issues of writing effectively for varying purposes, and that spell out lists of more specific skills such as punctuation, capitalization, spelling, sentence structure, and paragraph organization. One way to demonstrate to supervisors that district objectives are being addressed in classroom writing experiences is to include specific district objectives when developing the assessment checklists. Teachers could point out to colleagues the mandated curriculum objectives that are used.

Many school districts now require some more "objective" proof or demonstration of writing ability or competence. Many states have legislated requirements for measures of writing competency, and many school districts have worked to set up writing assessment procedures. One procedure now used in many settings (and one that is clearly preferable to using English usage scores from standardized tests and labeling them writing tests) is to elicit a writing sample from each student whose writing is to be assessed and then to rate each of the samples holistically, using a rating scale. Many school districts use holistic assessment, and districts have developed procedures for the collection and rating of samples. These procedures are summarized below (Myers, 1980).

One of the first tasks that must be undertaken is to create prompts for writing. Frequently, a group of teachers works to develop prompts that will stimulate fluent student writing. Prompts will vary according to the objectives and modes of writing (description, narration, exposition, report) being assessed. Students and teachers test prompts and suggest adjustments. To minimize the effects of topic choice on the quality of the writing, all students being assessed write a composition based on the same writing prompt.

A small group of teachers is selected to prepare the scoring criteria for writing samples. The teachers who participate in this preparation will be the table leaders at the subsequent district reading, where teachers will rate the compositions. This leader group is led by the single head reader. The table readers' first task is to select compositions that represent the scoring categories (for example, 1 through 6) that will be used in the final rating. To do this, the head reader asks the table leaders to read student compositions for an hour, selecting papers at random from the stack of compositions. The table leaders must identify two papers that could be used as anchors (pieces that typify a certain ranking) for each scoring category. If there are 6 categories, each table leader selects 12 pieces.

After selecting these anchors, the table leaders write down the characteristics that differentiate the ranking categories. The head reader then makes copies of the anchors selected by all of the table leaders and asks each table leader to read and score all of the copies and arrange them in a sequence on the table. The table leaders then vote on the scoring category for each anchor paper, discussing those on which there is disagreement and finally reaching a consensus on how to score each of the papers. The table leaders also discuss the range of papers that falls within each category. After these decisions have been made, the table leaders read for another hour, classifying more randomly selected papers into one category or another. This provides the table readers with the expertise needed to guide other teachers through the holistic procedure.

The head reader and the table leaders now take charge of the scoring of all the writing samples, the head reader running the reading session and the table leaders monitoring what happens at each table. Before they do the rating, the teachers participate in a training session designed to provide more consistency in rating. In the training session, teachers first receive a set of anchors along with instructions. They then rate each paper on a scale from 1 (the lowest score) to 6 (the highest score). When the teachers have completed this task, the head reader charts the scores that each teacher assigned to each composition. The group then examines those pieces that were rated most uniformly by the largest number of group members, seeking to find a typical 1, 2, 3, and so on. After agreeing on one set of anchors, the teachers follow the same procedure for a second set of anchors, this time giving more consideration to the papers in the middle categories and to papers that exemplify any problem trends identified by the table leaders or head reader. The teacher readers also discuss the differences between papers rated in different categories. The table leader takes notes on this discussion, and the head reader collects and summarizes the notes, which the teachers may then use as they read other compositions. These notes form the basis for rubrics, which describe the significant features of compositions in each scoring category.

Following this training, the raters are ready to rank the student compositions. The procedure for ranking the papers is the following: Two teachers read and rank each piece. The first teacher reads a paper and places it in front of his or her place. The table leader then gives the paper to another reader, who reads and scores it. The table leader examines the scores in order to compute a composite score. If the scores assigned are no more than one number apart, the two scores are added together and a composite score is given to the piece. If the scores assigned are more than one number apart, a third reader, usually the table leader, rates the composition. The table leaders change one of the original scores, moving the total score of the paper up or down, and that score becomes the composite score assigned to the composition.

Frequently, school districts decide to use holistic scoring for the purpose of determining minimal writing proficiency. In order to do this, the district (often through a mechanism such as a district proficiency committee) establishes a minimum composite score that must be achieved in order for the student to meet the district proficiency standard for graduation. Frequently, the committee makes its decision about a minimum composite after receiving a written report about the results of the district scoring sessions, along with samples of papers that represent each ranking (San Francisco Unified School District, 1987; Stack, 1988).

In addition to or as an alternative to holistic scoring, analytic rating imay be used. Aspects of writing— content, organization, vocabulary, grammar, and mechanics, each receive a separate score. Both ways of rating give an idea of the quality of the whole piece, without focus on discrete items (Samway, 1987a).

Holistic assessment has been welcomed by many educators because it involves teachers themselves in setting the standards for rankings, rather than the standards being imposed from the outside (Stack, 1988). But, as Samway (1987a, p. 297) notes, there are problems with this kind of holistic assessment.

After using this kind of tool with other teachers, Samway wrote,

> The holistic and categorical experiences did not allow the raters to peek into the greatness of each child. They had been asked to judge children based on a deficit model, rather than a best performance model. They were not asked to delineate what youngsters were able to do at that point in time and under certain conditions. In fact, they could not have done that as they did not have access to the wider context which had influenced the writing.

So while holistic rating of assigned writing might form a part of an assessment, it definitely should not replace the informal, observational strategies described earlier.

Summary

Assessment of writing is an issue that must be faced by all teachers, whether they work in native language or ESL settings. Therefore, teachers must have a clear view of assessment procedures. This chapter makes the following points about the issue of assessment:

1) Assessment should be based on observation and documentation of what children are doing in authentic classroom writing contexts.
2) Classroom teachers should use a variety of methods for observing and documenting children's writing. These methods may include close observation of individual children, collection of children's work in writing folders, and documentation of children's progress through anecdotal records and checklists. An essential part of teaching writing is keeping records of children's development over time.

3) The learners themselves should be involved in reflecting on their own progress as writers.

4) Teachers need to be prepared to share with parents and supervisors the work that they are doing with children and the progress children are making.

5) School districts that are concerned about measuring students' writing competence may want to consider using holistic assessments of writing samples rather than standardized tests.

Conclusion

With the changes that have come about in our understanding of the writing process, educators have changed many of their teaching practices. This has been true both in native language and in ESL settings. But, as Bailey et al. (1988) point out, changes in the ways that schools assess and report student writers' strengths and needs must also occur to a much greater extent than they have in the past.

We have been conditioned to using traditional language generated from scope-and-sequence charts. We have continued to use those descriptors, redefining them in our minds to fit a meaning-centered approach, but forgetting that the traditional connotations would be a part of the messages that would be received by other professionals and parents unless we totally revise the way we report in a meaning-based reading and writing program.

> From " Problem Solving Our Way to Alternative Evaluation Procedures" by J. Bailey et al., *Language Arts, 65 (4)* p. 366. Copyright (1988) by National Council of Teachers of English. Used with permission.

The assessment of children's writing and of children's progress as writers is complex and multifaceted, as is the teaching of writing. The assessment strategies described here reflect attempts to make major changes.

References

Allen, V. (1986). Developing contexts to support second language acquisition. *Language Arts, 63,* 61-66.

Allen, V., & Hudelson, S. (1986). *Talking and writing: Helping LEP students make the connection.* Paper presented at the annual convention of Teachers of English to Speakers of Other Languages, Anaheim.

Alvarez, L. (1988). *Pursuing collaboration: One's project's odyssey.* Paper presented at the annual convention of Teachers of English to Speakers of Other Languages, Chicago, March.

Applebee, A., Auten, A., & Lehr, F. (1981). *Writing in the secondary school: English and the content areas.* Urbana, IL: National Council of Teachers of English.

Atwell, N. (1987). *In the middle.* Portsmouth, NH: Heinemann.

Au, K. (1980). Participation structures in a reading lesson with Hawaiian children: Analysis of a culturally appropriate instructional event. *Anthropology & Education Quarterly, 11,* 91-115.

Baghban, M. (1984). *Our daughter learns to read and write.* Newark, DE: International Reading Association. (ERIC Document Reproduction Service No. 248 496.)

Bailey, J., Brazee, P., Chiavaroli, S., Herbeck, J., Lechner, T., Lewis, D., McKittrick, A., Redwine, L., Reid, K., Robinson, B., & Spear, H. (1988). Problem solving our way to alternative evaluation procedures. *Language Arts, 65,* 364-74.

Barnitz, J. (1985). *Reading development of nonnative speakers of English.* Orlando, FL: Harcourt, Brace, & Jovanovich. (ERIC Document Reproduction Service No. 256 182.)

Bartelo, D.M. (1984). *Getting the picture of reading and writing: A look at the drawings, composing and oral language of limited English proficiency children.* Alexandria, VA: United States Department of Education, (ERIC Document Reproduction Service No. 245 533.)

Berthoff, A. (1981). *The making of meaning.* Upper Montclair, NJ : Boynton Cook.

Bird, L., & Alvarez, L. (1987). Beyond comprehension: The power of literature study for language minority students. *TESOL in Elementary Education Newsletter, 10,* 1-2.

Bissex, G. (1980). *GNYS AT WRK.* Cambridge, MA: Harvard University Press.

Britton, J. (1970). *Language and learning.* Coral Gables, FL: University of Miami Press. (ERIC Document Reproduction Service No. 052 217.)

Britton, J., Burgess, T., Martin, N., McLeod, A., & Rosen, H. (1975). *The development of writing abilities.* London: Macmillan Education Ltd. (ERIC Document Reproduction Service No. 144 049.)

Bruner, J. (1981). The pragmatics of acquisition. In W. Deutsch (Ed.), *The child's construction of language.* New York: Academic Press.

Calkins, L. (1983). *Lessons from a child.* Exeter, NH: Heinemann. (ERIC Document Reproduction Service No. 263 614.)

Calkins, L. (1986). *The art of teaching writing.* Portsmouth, NH: Heinemann. (ERIC Document Reproduction Service No. 263 613.)

Carle, E. (1969). *The very hungry cat.* New York: World Publishing Company.

Cathcart-Strong, R. (1986). Input generation by young second language learners. *TESOL Quarterly, 20,* 515-530.

Cazden, C. (1986). ESL teachers as language advocates for children. In P. Rigg & D. S. Enright (Eds.), *Children and ESL: Integrating perspectives.* Washington, DC: Teachers of English to Speakers of Other Languages.

Charlip, R. (1964). *Fortunately.* New York: Macmillan.

Chamot, A.U., & O'Malley, M. (1987). The cognitive academic language learning approach: A bridge to the mainstream. *TESOL Quarterly, 21,* 227-250.

Clay, M. (1975). *What did I write? Beginning writing behavior.* Auckland, N.Z.: Heinemann. (ERIC Document Reproduction Service No. 264 571.)

Crandall, J. (Ed.). (1987). *ESL through content-area instruction.* Englewood Cliffs, NJ: Prentice-Hall. (ERIC Document Reproduction Service No. 283 387.)

Crawford, J. (1987). Bilingual education: Language, learning and politics. *EducationWeek,* April 1, 19-50.

DeFord, D. (1981). Literacy: Reading, writing and other essentials. *Language Arts, 58,* 652-659.

DeFord, D, & Harste, J. (1982). Child language research and curriculum. *Language*

Arts, 59, 590-600.

Delgado-Gaitan, C. (1987). Mexican adult literacy: New directions for immigrants. In S. Goldman & H. Trueba (Eds.), *Becoming literate in English as a second language*. Norwood, NJ: Ablex Publishing Company.

DeRegniers, B. (1965). *May I bring a friend?* New York: Atheneum.

Doake, D. (1985). Reading-like behavior: Its role in learning to read. In A. Jaggar & M.T. Smith-Burke (Eds.), *Observing the language learner*. Newark, DE: International Reading Association; and Urbana, IL: National Council of Teachers of English. (ERIC Document Reproduction Service No. 251 857.)

Dulay, H., & Burt, M. (1974). A new perspective on the creative construction process in child second language acquisition. *Language Learning, 24*, 253-278.

Dyson, A. (1982). The emergence of visible language: Interrelationships between drawing and early writing. *Visible Language, 16*, 360-381.

Dyson, A. (1984). Learning to write/learning to do school: Emergent writers' interpretations of school literacy tasks. *Research in the Teaching of English, 18*, 233-264.

Dyson, A. (1987). Individual differences in beginning composing: An orchestral vision of learning to compose. *Written Communication, 4*, 411-442.

Edelsky, C. (1982). Writing in a bilingual program: The relation of L1 and L2 texts. *TESOL Quarterly, 16*, 211-228.

Edelsky, C. (1983). Segmentation and punctuation: Developmental data from young writers in a bilingual program. *Research in the Teaching of English, 17*, 135-156.

Edelsky, C. (1986). *Writing in a bilingual program: Habia una vez*. Norwood, NJ: Ablex Publishing.

Edelsky, C. (in press-a). Bilingual children's writing: Fact and fiction. In D. Johnson & D. Roen (Eds.), *Richness in writing: Empowering ESL students*. New York: Longman.

Edelsky, C. (in press-b). Coming to understand whole language: What was spotlighted; what was left in the wings. To appear in L.B. Bird (Ed.), *Becoming a whole language school*. New York: Richard C. Owen Press.

Edelsky, C. (in press-c). Living in the author's world: Analyzing the author's craft. To appear in *California Reading Journal*.

Edelsky, C., & Jilbert, C. (1985). Bilingual children and writing: Lessons for all of us. *Volta Review, 87*, 57-72.

Edelsky, C., & Hudelson, S. (1987). *Contextual complexities: Written language policies for bilingual programs*. Berkeley, CA: Center for the Study of Writing.

Ellis, R. (1985). *Understanding second language acquisition*. New York: Oxford University Press.

Emig, J. (1971). The composing process of twelfth graders. Urbana, IL: National Council of Teachers of English (ERIC Document Reproduction Service No. 058 205.)

Enright, D.S. (1986). Use everything you have to teach English: Providing useful input to young language learners. In P. Rigg & D.S. Enright (Eds.), *Children and ESL: Integrating perspectives*. Washington, DC: Teachers of English to Speakers of Other Languages.

Enright, D. S., & McCloskey, M. (1988). Yes talking! : Organizing the classroom to promote seconf language acquisition. *TESOL Quarterly, 19*, 431 - 453.

Enright, D.S., & McCloskey, M. (1988). *Integrating English: Developing English language and literacy in multilingual classrooms*. Reading, MA: Addison-Wesley.

Ferreiro, E., & Teberosky, A. (1982). *Literacy before schooling*. Portsmouth, NH: Heinemann. (ERIC Document Reproduction Service No. 263 542.)

Fillmore, L. (1976). *The second time around: Cognitive and social strategies in second language acquisition*. Unpublished doctoral dissertation, Stanford University, Stanford, CA.

Fillmore, L. (1983). The language learner as an individual: Implications of research on individual differences for the ESL teacher. In J. Handscombe & M. Clarke (Eds.), *On TESOL '82: Pacific perspectives on language learning and teaching*. Washington, DC: Teachers of English to Speakers of Other Languages.

Fillmore, L. (1986). Equity or excellence. *Language Arts, 63*, 474-481.

Flores, B., & Garcia, E. (1984). A collaborative learning and teaching experience using journals. *NABE Journal, 8*, 67-83.

Flores, B., Garcia, E., Gonzalez, S., Hidalgo, G., Kaczmarek, K., & Romero, T. (1985). *Bilingual holistic instructional strategies*. Chandler, AZ: Exito.

Florio, S., & Clark, C.M. (1982). The functions of writing in an elementary classroom. *Research in the teaching of English , 16*, 115-130.

Flower, L., & Hayes, J. (1981). A cognitive process theory of writing. *College Composition and Communication, 32,* 365-387.

Franklin, E. (1986). Literacy instruction for LEP children. *Language Arts, 63,* 51-59.

Freeman, Y., & Freeman, D. (in press). Whole language approaches to writing with secondary ESL students. In D. Johnson & D. Roen (Eds.), *Richness in writing: Empowering ESL students.* New York: Longman.

Fulwiler, T. (Ed.). (1987). *The journal book.* Portsmouth, NH: Boynton/Cook Publishers. (ERIC Document Reproduction Service No. 284 296.)

Genesee, F. (1987). *Learning through two languages.* Rowley, MA: Newbury House.

Genishi, C., & Dyson, A. (1984). *Language assessment in the early years.* Norwood, NJ: Ablex Publishing. (ERIC Document Reproduction Service No. 265 554.)

Gomez, I. (1985). *From talk to text: The role of peer conferences in elementary ESL student's writing.* Unpublished paper.

Goodman, K. (1967). Reading: A psycholinguistic guessing game. *Journal of the Reading Specialist, 4,* 126-135.

Goodman, K., & Goodman, Y. (1979). Learning to read is natural. In L. Resnick & P. Weaver (Eds.), *Theory and practice of early reading.* Hillsdale, NJ: Lawrence Erlbaum and Associates.

Goodman, Y. (1986). Children coming to know literacy. In W. Teale & E. Sulzby (Eds.), *Emergent literacy: Writing and reading.* Norwood, NJ: Ablex Publishing .

Goodman, Y., and Altwerger, B. (1981). *Print awareness in preschool children: A study of the development of literacy in preschool children.* (Occasional Paper No 4). Tucson, AZ: University of Arizona, Program in Language and Literacy, Arizona Center for Research and Development, College of Education.
(ERIC Document Reproduction Service No. 210 629.)

Graves, D. (1983). *Writing: Teachers and children at work.* Exeter, NH: Heinemann. (ERIC Document Reproduction Service No. 234 430.)

Graves, D. (1984). *A researcher learns to write.* Portsmouth, NH: Heinemann.

Hakuta, K. (1986). *Mirror of language: The debate on bilingualism.* New York: Basic Books. (ERIC Document Reproduction Service No. 264 326.)

Halliday, M. (1973). *Explorations in the functions of language.* London: Edward

Arnold. (ERIC Document Reproduction Service No. 095 550.)

Halsell, S. (1986). *An ethnographic account of the composing behaviors of five young bilingual students.* Paper presented at the annual meeting of the American Educational Research Association, San Francisco.

Hansen, J., Newkirk, T., & Graves, D. (Eds.). (1985). *Breaking ground: Teachers relate reading and writing in the elementary school.* Portsmouth, NH: Heinemann. (ERIC Document Reproduction Service No. 257 050.)

Harste, J., Woodward, V., & Burke, C. (1984). *Language stories and literacy lessons.* Portsmouth, NH: Heinemann. (ERIC Document Reproduction Service No. 257 113.)

Hayes, C.W., & Bahruth, B. (1985a). Querer es poder. In J. Hansen, T. Newkirk, & D. Graves (Eds.), *Breaking ground: Teachers relate reading and writing in the elementary school.* Portsmouth, NH: Heinemann.

Hayes, C.W., Bahruth, B., & Kessler, C. (1985b). *To read you must write: Children in language acquisition.* Paper presented at the International Conference on Second/Foreign Language Acquisition by Children. (ERIC Document Reproduction Service No. ED 257 313.)

Heald-Taylor, G. (1987). Predictable literature selections and activities for language arts instruction. *Reading Teacher, 41,* 6-13.

Heath, S.B. (1983). *Ways with words.* Cambridge: Cambridge University Press.

Heath, S.B. (1985). Literacy or literate skills. In P. Larsen, E. Judd, D. Messerschnitt (Eds.), *On TESOL '84: A brave new world.* Washington, DC: Teachers of English to Speakers of Other Languages. (ERIC Document Reproduction No. 274 168.)

Heath. S.B. (1986). *Learners at risk.* Plenary address presented at the Twentieth Annual Convention of the Teachers of English to Speakers of Other Languages, Anaheim, March.

Hilgers, T. (1986). How children change as critical evaluators of writing: Four three-year case studies. *Research in the Teaching of English, 20,* 36-55.

Hudelson, S. (1981-82). An examination of children's invented spelling in Spanish. *National Association for Bilingual Education Journal, 6,* 53-68.

Hudelson, S. (1984). Can yu ret an rayt en ingles: Children become literate in English as a second language. *TESOL Quarterly, 18,* 221-238.

Hudelson, S. (1986). Children's writing in ESL: What we've learned, what we're learning. In P. Rigg & D.S. Enright (Eds.), *Children and ESL: Integrating perspectives.* Washington, DC: Teachers of English to Speakers of Other Languages.

Hudelson, S. (1987). The role of native language literacy in the education of language minority children. *Language Arts, , 64,* 827-84

Hudelson, S. (1988a). *Bilingual learners in the English classroom.* Manuscript submitted for publication.

Hudelson, S. (1988b). "Teaching" English through content area activities. Manuscript submitted for publication.

Hudelson, S. (in press). A tale of two children: Individual differences in second language writing. In D. Johnson & D. Roen (Eds.), *Richness in writing: Empowering ESL students.* New York: Longman.

Irvine, P., & Spolsky, B. (1980). Sociolinguistic aspects of acceptance of literacy in the vernacular. In R. Barkin & E. Brandt (Eds.), *Speaking, singing and teaching: A multidisciplinary approach to language variation.* Tempe, AZ: Arizona State University, Anthropological Research Papers No. 20.

Jacobs, S. (1984). Investigative writing: Practice and principles. *Language Arts, 61,* 365-363.

Kinneavy, J. (1971). *A universe of discourse.* Englewood Cliffs, NJ: Prentice Hall.

Kitagawa, C., & Kitagawa, M. (1987). *Making connections with writing: An expressive writing model in Japanese schools.* Portsmouth, NH: Heinemann. (ERIC Document Reproduction Service No. 282 225.)

Kitagawa, M. (in press). Letting ourselves be taught. In D. Johnson & D. Roen (Eds.), *Richness in writing: Empowering ESL students.* New York: Longman.

Krashen, S. (1982). *Principles and practices in second language acquisition.* New York: Pergamon Press.

Krauss, R. (1945). *The carrot seed.* New York: Harper & Row.

Kreeft, J., Shuy, R., Staton, J., Reed, L., & Morroy, R. (1984). *Dialogue journal writing: Analysis of student-teacher interactive writing in the learning of English as a second language.* National Institute of Education (NIE-G-83-0030). Washington, DC: Center for Applied Linguistics. (ERIC Document Reproduction Service No. 252 097.)

Kreeft, J. (1984). The importance of teacher questions in written interactions. In J.

Kreeft et al., (Eds.) *Dialogue journal writing: Analysis of student-teacher interactive writing in the learning of English as a second language.* National Institute of Education (NIE-G-83-0030). Washington, DC: Center for Applied Linguistics. (ERIC Document Reproduction Service No. 252 097.)

Lamme, L.L., & Childers, N.M. (1983). The composing processes of three young children. *Research in the Teaching of English, 15,* 113-134.

Lindfors, J. (1987). *Children's language and learning* (2nd ed.). Englewood Cliffs, NJ: Prentice Hall.

Lindfors, J. (1988a). From "talking together" to "being together in talk." *Language Arts, 65,* 135-141.

Lindfors, J. (1988b). Zulu students' questioning in dialogue journals. *Questioning Exchange, 2,* 1-16.

Mohan, B. (1986). *Language and content.* Reading, MA: Addison-Wesley.

Myers, M. (1980). *A procedure for writing assessment.* Urbana, IL: National Council of Teachers of English. (ERIC Document Reproduction Service No. 193 676.)

Nations, M. (1986). *Making use of available resources for writing.* Unpublished paper, Georgia State University.

Newkirk, T. (1984). Archimedes' dream. *Language Arts, 61,* 341-350.

Ochs, E. & Schieffelen, B. (1983). *Language acquisition and socialization: Three developmental stories and their implications.* (Sociolinguistic Working Paper No. 105). Austin, TX: Southwest Educational Development Laboratory. (ERIC Document Reproduction Service No. 252 065.)

Oljean, V. (1984). The dual function of narrative in writing. *Language Arts, 61,* 376-382.

Perl, S. (1979). The composing processes of unskilled college writers. *Research in the teaching of English, 13,* 317-336.

Perl, S., & Wilson, N. (1986). *Through teachers' eyes: Portraits of writing teachers at work.* Portsmouth, NH: Heinemann.

Peyton, J.K. (1987). *Dialogue journal writing with limited-English-proficient students.* Washington, DC: ERIC Clearinghouse on Languages and Linguistics. (ERIC Document Reproduction Service No. 287 308.)

Peyton, J.K. (1988). *Beginning at the beginning: First grade ESL students learn to write.*

Manuscript submitted for publication.

Peyton, J.K. & Mackinson-Smyth, J. (in press). Writing and talking about writing: Computer networking with elementary students. In D. Johnson & D. Roen (Eds.), *Richness in writing: Empowering ESL students.* New York: Longman.

Philips. S. (1983). *The invisible culture.* New York: Longman. (ERIC Document Reproduction Service No. 226 878.)

Piazza, C. (1987). Identifying context variables in research on writing: A review and suggested directions. *Written Communication, 4,* 107-137.

Piper, T. (1986). *Stories and the teaching of language in a grade two ESL class.* Paper presented at the Annual Meeting of the National Council of Teachers of English, San Antonio. (ERIC Document Reproduction Service No. 278 268.)

Read, C. (1971). Pre-school children's knowledge of English phonology. *Harvard Educational Review, 41,* 1-34.

Read, C. (1975). *Children's categorization of speech sounds.* Urbana, IL: National Council of Teachers of English. (ERIC Document Reproduction Service No. 112 426.)

Reed, L. (1984). Dialogue journals: An important classroom management tool. In J. Kreeft, R. Shuy, J. Staton, L. Reed, & R. Morroy (Eds.) *Dialogue writing: Analysis of student-teacher interactive writing in the learning of English as a second Language.* National Institute of Education Grant (NIE-G-83-0030). Washington, DC: Center for Applied Linguistics (ERIC Document Reproduction Service ED 252 097.)

Rhodes, L. (1981). I can read: Predictable books as resources for reading and writing instruction. *Reading Teacher, 34,* 511-518.

Rigg, P., & Enright, D.S. (Eds.). (1986). *Children and ESL: Integrating perspectives.* Washington, DC: Teachers of English to Speakers of Other Languages.

Samway, K. (1987a). Formal evaluation of children's writing: An incomplete story. *Language Arts, 64,* 289-298.

Samway, K. (1987b). *The writing processes of non-native English speaking children in the elementary grades.* Unpublished doctoral dissertation, University of Rochester, Rochester, NY.

Samway, K., & Alvarez, L. (1987). Integrating language arts instruction for language minority students. *Educational Horizons, 66,* 20-19.
San Francisco Unified School District. (1987). *Wholistic Scoring Packet.* California

Assessment Program. Writing Assessment.

Schieffelin, B., & Cochran-Smith, M. (1984). Learning to read culturally: Literacy before schooling. In H. Goelman, A. Oberg, & F. Smith (Eds.), *Awakening to literacy*. Portsmouth, NH: Heinemann.

Searfoss, L., Smith, C., & Bean, T. (1981). An integrated strategy for second language learners. *TESOL Quarterly, 15*, 383-392.

Shuy, R. (1982). Analysis of language functions in dialogue journal writing. In J. Staton, R. Shuy, & J. Kreeft. (Eds.), *Analysis of dialogue journal writing as a communicative event*. Final Report to the National Institute of Education (NIE-G-80-0122). (ERIC Document Reproduction Service No. 214 196.)

Shuy, R. (1984). The function of language functions in the dialogue journal interactions of nonnative English speakers and their teachers. In J. Kreeft, R. Shuy, J. Staton, L. Reed, & R. Morroy (Eds.), *Dialogue writing: Analysis of student-teacher interactive writing in the learning of English as a second language*. National Institute of Education Grant (NIE-G-83-0030). Washington, DC: Center for Applied Linguistics (ERIC Document Reproduction Service ED 252 097.)

Smith, F. (1982). *Writing and the writer*. New York: Holt, Rinehart and Winston.

Stack, J. (1988). *Holistic evaluation of student writing*. Session presented at the Twenty-second Annual Convention of Teachers of English to Speakers of Other Languages, Chicago, March.

Staton, J. (1984). Dialogue journals as a means of enabling written language acquisition. In J. Kreeft, R. Shuy, J. Staton, L. Reed, & R. Morroy, (Eds.), *Dialogue writing: Analysis of student-teacher interactive writing in the learning of English as a second language*. National Institute of Education Grant (NIE-G-83-0030). Washington, DC: Center for Applied Linguistics (ERIC Document Reproduction Service ED 252 097.)

Strong, M. (1983). Social Styles and the second language acquisition of Spanish-speaking kindergartners. In *TESOL Quarterly, 17*, 241-258.

Sulzby, E. (1986). Writing and reading: Signs of oral and written language organization in the young child. In W. Teale and E. Sulzby (Eds.), *Emergent literacy: Writing and reading*. Norwood, NJ: Ablex Publishing. (ERIC Document Reproduction Service No. 280 004.)

Taylor, D. (1983). *Family literacy: Young children learning to read and write*. Portsmouth, NH: Heinemann. (ERIC Document Reproduction Service No. 264 526.)

Taylor, D., & Dorsey-Gaines, C. (1988). *Growing up literate: Learning from inner-city families*. Portsmouth, NH: Heinemann.

Teale, W., and Sulzby, E. (1986). *Emergent literacy: Writing and reading*. Norwood, NJ: Ablex Publishing. (ERIC Document Reproduction Service No. 280 004.)

Urzua, C. (1986). A children's story. In P. Rigg & D.S. Enright (Eds.), *Children and ESL: Integrating perspectives*. Washington, DC: Teachers of English to Speakers of Other Languages.

Urzua, C. (1987a). *Empowering learners through whole-language teaching/learning*. Speech delivered at the Annual Meeting of California Teachers of English to Speakers of Other Languages, Pasadena.

Urzua, C. (1987b). 'You stopped too soon': Second language children composing and revising. *TESOL Quarterly, 21*, 279-304.

Ventriglia, L. (1982). *Conversations of Miguel and Maria: How children learn a second language*. Reading, MA: Addison-Wesley.

Watkins-Goffman, K. (1987). *A case study of second language writing process of a sixth grade writing group*. Unpublished doctoral dissertation, New York University.

Wells, G. (1986). *The meaning makers: Children's learning language and using language to learn*. Portsmouth, NH: Heinemann. (ERIC Document Reproduction Service No. 264 572.)